CHRISTIAN COUNSELING

Dr. STEVEN BENAVIDES

A new path to integral healing.

Copyright Esteban Benavides
Christhian Counseling, 2026

The reproduction of this book or parts of it in any form, or its storage on a system or transmission in any way or by any electronic, mechanical, photocopy or other means is not authorized without prior written permission from the author.

Published in Spanish under the title:
Consejería Cristiana, 2023.
Editorial Pan House

English Version: RCM Producciones

ÍNDICE

Dedication 7
Acknowledgements 9
ForewordOREWORD 11
COMMENTS 13

I.
THE IDEA OF COUNSELING AND
THE THEORIES OF HUMAN DEVELOPMENT 15

Notions about Counseling 17
Biological developmental theory and Sigmund Freud 18
Alfred Adler's social development theory. 26
Carl Rogers and Albert Ellis' cognitive development theory. 31

II.
COUNSELING SESSION: WHAT IT IS AND MORE 37

Establishing the relationship 39
Identifying the problem 41
Taking action 42
Ending the counseling session 43
Bibliotherapy as a stand-alone format 45
Step 1: Identifying the patient's primary concerns 45
Step 2: Determining session objectives 45
Step 3: Conducting Research 45
Step 4: Reading and examining all identified materials 46
Step 5: Assessing biases and opinions and identifying
        potential triggers 46
Step 6: Setting the stage, provide a safe learning
        environment, perception 46
Step 7: Providing guidance and homework 46

Step 8: Ongoing sessions and referrals 46
Classic counseling model with an emphasis
on bibliotherapy 48

III.
CREATION OF COMMUNITY COUNSELING
CENTERS WITH CHRISTIAN VALUES. 49

1. Assessment of community needs and objectives 52
2. Trained and professional staff 52
3. Infrastructure and resources 52
4. Comprehensive Care Approach 53
5. Collaboration with local churches and
   Christian organizations 53
6. Cultural sensitivity and inclusion Creating
   Virtual Counseling Centers with Christian Values 54
1. Develop a comprehensive and achievable plan 54
2. Technology and Platform Selection 54
3. Recruiting and training counselors 54
4. Establishing an outreach strategy 55
5. Incorporate Christian principles 55
6. Focus on accessibility and inclusion 55

IV.
FAMILY AND COUNSELING. 57

The role of the father 59
Fundamental principles governing the role of a father
and family man from the perspective of a counselor 59
The role of a mother 61
Fundamental principles governing the role of a mother
and a family woman from the perspective of a counselor 61
Benefits of a family with both parents 63
Advantages of raising children in a family with both parents 63
The divorce 64

V.
THE COUNSELING RESPONSE: .CASE STUDIES. 67

Grief 69
Suicide 72
Divorce...75
Divorce and remarriage..76
Substance abuse 78
Pornography Addiction..79
Abortion 81
Violence against women..83
Psychological or sexual abuse/rape against women...................84
Sexual identity and gender 87
Sexual identity or gender...88

VI.
REAL-LIFE CASES OF APLIED COUNSELING. 91

First experience:
Grief and ethics...93
Exercise 95
Second experience:
Abortion and a Christian perspective..96
Third experience:
From drug addict to pastor 97
Introduction to the Counseling Model..98
Integral Biblical Development (IBD)
 by Dr. Steven Benavides...98
Counseling Model 99
References 101

DEDICATION

To my mother, Lupita Adame de Benavides.

She taught me to love education and wisdom.

ACKNOWLEDGEMENTS

To my book team:

To Dr. Leonardo Gutiérrez M., translator, editor, photographer, confident and companion for coffee and long nights. We did it, Leon!

To my educators:

Mrs. Carr, my fourth-grade teacher, who gave me a Fig Bar for every perfect grade and taught me that I was smart.

To Mrs. Yates, my high school journalism teacher. She taught me that we are all equal regardless of race or color.

To Mrs. Karen Zeissel, my high school speech teacher. She nurtured me to follow my convictions and was a true in loco parentis.

Thanks to Dr. Don Thorsen, my theology teacher, who taught me how to defend my faith.

Likewise, to Dr. Alma Garcia, my counseling professor. She taught me to honor and respect the counseling process.

To my family:

To Frances, my beautiful wife of thirty-four years. We have lived a lot of life, but I want even more by your side. Thank you for our children and all your sacrifice. I love you more than when you were eighteen.

To Steven III, Bethany Celeste, Matthew Ryan and Paul Jaden, our children. They are my pride, love, joy and hope.

To Dr. Esteban R. Benavides, my dad, my hero, and to Mrs. Guadalupe Adame de Benavides, my mom, my first love.

To Guadalupe, Efrén, Merari, and Eliú, my siblings. They are the wind under my wings, my friends, my memories, and my laughter.

My church family. There are so many of you! I love you all.

To my students. I have learned a lot from you. Thank you for your contributions to this project. Keep learning better questions.

FOREWORD

In the vast landscape of counseling, where the paths of psychology and spirituality intersect, we delve into the pages of this work with Doctor Steven Benavides. This book is a lighthouse that illuminates the path of Christian and non-Christian counseling as a tool for integral healing.

Dr. Benavides guides us through the twists and turns of counseling, where biblical wisdom and scientific evidence-based psychological techniques are intertwined. In your approach, we recognize the importance of considering the spiritual dimension as a fundamental component of mental and emotional health.

From the fundamentals of the counselor's work to the analysis of different theories of psychosocial development, this book provides a rich and balanced perspective on counseling. Through practical cases, it shows us how to establish relationships of trust, identify central problems, and take concrete measures for healing.

Beyond theories and techniques, Dr. Benavides urges us to understand and address everyday problems that require counseling, from grief to addictions, through issues of sexual identity and gender violence. In each of these cases, we find practical recommendations and an ethical compass that guides the counselor in his work.

Christian counseling, as presented in these pages, is distinguished by its integral approach, its foundation in the Scriptures, and its emphasis on prayer as a therapeutic practice.

On this journey, the Christian counselor emerges as an agent of change, a lighthouse of hope, and a model of service. He is expected, not only to have knowledge, but also empathy, authenticity and a congruence between his discourse and its praxis. His work, though challenging, is immensely valuable to those seeking healing and guidance.

This book is a reminder that counseling is an evolving discipline. The integration of Christian principles with conventional therapeutic methods is a promising path, but not without challenges. The search for a balance between faith and professional ethics, respect for cultural diversity and the need for constant research are part of the journey.

Ultimately, this work invites us to reflect on the importance of counseling in a world that often feels fragmented and wounded. It reminds us that there will always be those who need a counselor, and there will always be a guide willing to serve humanity. That guide is the counselor, and this book is a compass for their way.

May these pages be a source of inspiration and wisdom for all counselors and a lighthouse of hope for those seeking healing and renewal in their personal journey.

Ray Corea
CEO RCM Comunicaciones
Pastor / Writer / Coach

COMMENTS

"The complexity of the human mind, soul and spirit may seem overwhelming to most. Dr. Steven Benavides, through his extensive literature, has produced a coherent and ambitious text on the subject and practice of psychology from both, a Christian and secular perspective. His passion and dedication to teaching and equipping people for deeper understanding are inspiring. His book provides the reader with tools and resources to help them through difficult life stages. Written from a Christian perspective, Dr. Benavides challenges his audience to grow, pursue and embrace life".

Ruby Garza LMFT
Marriage and family therapist

"The book Christian Counseling: A New Path to Integral Healing, written by Dr. Benavides, offers a valuable perspective on how to combine Christian principles with psychological techniques to provide holistic spiritual and emotional support to people facing various life situations.

The author presents a holistic approach that recognizes the importance of addressing both the spiritual and emotional needs of individuals. Through his deep knowledge of psychology and Christian faith, Dr. Benavides proposes a counseling model that seeks to harmonize these two aspects of human life.

This book is an integrated model for spiritual and emotional support. It is an essential guide for Christian counselors, religious leaders and anyone interested in understanding how psychology and faith can work together to provide effective support in difficult times. It offers a comprehensive and practical view of how to help people find hope and restoration in their spiritual and emotional journey."

Dr. David Lazo
Ministry Unidos en Amor.
Elevating Marriages to Another Level

"In this Christian counseling book, Dr. Steven Benavides shares methods of counseling that are profound yet easily adapted to a general or specialized audience. Spiritual counseling is evident and integral to the concepts of psychological and spiritual integration.

Dr. Benavides, as a bicultural and bilingual teacher, is passionate about biblical and psychological scholarship. His concepts embrace cross-cultural terms and bridges or learning methods that are among the few that make this work a true excellence.

The material in this book is organized to provide spiritual and academic information to church and secular audiences. It is suitable for leadership conferences, biblical institutions, leadership trainings and much more. The book is a must-read for the casual and serious reader of psychological and religious integration in counseling today."

Dr. Elías Garza, Jr.
Senior Pastor
CCC Weslaco

"The World Health Organization defines that a complete state of health is not only physical, but also psychological. Through the pages of this book, you will learn the determinant goals to achieve good mental health.

The neurochemical processes are something difficult for doctors to treat; that is why people like Dr. Steven Benavides are essential for the correct expression of ideas of this XXI century".

Dr. David Pérez
Medical Surgeon

"Dr. Benavides has put together in this work a mosaic of useful proposals to confront the growing tendency in the crises of the human being. A solid academic background and a very broad experience in the practical field are the foundation to structure in this book a model of counseling accessible to the lay reader or the active minister. Dr. Benavides is a qualified interpreter of the Scriptures and is aware of contemporary challenges, which coincides in his expertise to impress his readers with the biblical message of inner healing and abundant life. This book in your hands has the potential to reach beyond your reading."

Dr. Leonardo Gutiérrez M.
Pastor Counselor

I

THE IDEA OF COUNSELING AND THE THEORIES OF HUMAN DEVELOPMENT

NOTIONS ABOUT COUNSELING

Have you ever wondered if counseling could be a more structured resource for psychosocial support?

For centuries, counseling has been a very kind and empathetic way for human beings to support one another. It often happens that we are unsure of what decision to make at a given moment, and another person, who sees things more clearly than we do, has the potential to help us understand what we cannot see simply because we are overwhelmed by a situation that affects us very personally. The other person, who sees things from the outside, may have a more objective view of the matter and therefore possess more intuition, conviction, and certainty.

Most of the time, we believe that giving advice is simply expressing a personal opinion in order to guide or direct someone who is desperate toward a certain path that seems to be the most appropriate, and yes, this is true, but what is counseling really? Could it also be a more specialized human work strategy? Let's see.

Well, counseling is essentially an agreement between an individual with emotional problems and a counselor who tries to identify goals and potential solutions. Its overall purpose is emotional stability, promoting interpersonal communication skills, helping to develop coping skills, improving self-esteem, and promoting positive changes in behavior and mental health.

First, the process involves establishing trust and confidentiality. It is important that both parties show mutual respect when entering an effective counseling relationship, since without discretion, one of the most important qualities of counseling is lost. That said, we can now get down to business.

Counseling is more than just a voluntary human act; it can also be a field of study with a powerful scope and incredible potential for human assistance. In order to make it even more effective, it has foundations or theories that guide the counselor.

The study of psychology normally divides these foundations or principles into biological, social, or cognitive theories. In modern psychology and current counseling practice, a combination of theoretical foundations is often used, which gives it a broader scope and converges into a strategy that combines theoretical principles and practices for a more holistic and even spiritual application. In my opinion, it is optimal for the counselor to use the theories that are most applicable to the case, the setting, and the population being studied.

Now, we can talk about three original thinkers who have shaped counseling psychology. Dr. Sigmund Freud, known as the leading figure in biological psychology. His concepts have led him to be labeled the father of modern psychology, and his contribution to counseling identifies him as someone who views human development through a biological lens. Although some today would consider him outdated, his arguments on sexual identity and gender place him back at the center of contemporary psychological dialogue.

On the other hand, Dr. Alfred Adler, Freud's contemporary and colleague, took a broader view of human development. He proposed that development is not only a biological phenomenon but should be seen through a wide range of social influences. His perspectives on psychology and his theses on human development generally identify him as a social theorist who seeks to view human development as part of the social and family influences that affect the individual.

Finally, the third basis of developmental theories is very well defined by Dr. Carl Rogers and Dr. Albert Ellis. They are considered the most important theorists in the field of cognitive development. Why do I think it is crucial to discuss these theories in relation to counseling? Because, in this case, human cognitive development is based on the inherent growth of human beings in the process of acquiring the ability to organize knowledge and use it to bring about changes in their physical, mental, and emotional development. These changes lead human beings to develop their memory, to solve problems effectively, to apply reasoning, and to perform bodily functions correctly.

Biological developmental theory and Sigmund Freud

Sigmund Freud, an Austrian neurologist and pioneer of psychoanalysis, proposed theories of psychology and human development that dominated subsequent studies in psychology. Freud's theories on human development explore the different stages of growth, the role of unconscious motivations, and explain how early experiences shape an individual's growth.

Freud's psychosexual development model reveals that the human psyche is made up of three main parts: the id, the ego, and the superego. This section will examine Freud's fundamental principles and explore how significant they are in counseling and psychotherapy.

First, Freud's theories on human growth and development begin with the concept of personality structures: the id, the ego, and the superego. The "id" is the primitive, unconscious part of the psyche that seeks immediate gratification of desires and needs. The "ego" acts as a mediator between the desires of the id and external reality. The "superego" is the moral conscience that imposes ideals of right and wrong on our behavior.

Freud explains that, at an early age, children's behaviors are dominated by the id, characterized by a primary interest in oral, anal, and genital pleasure centers. As children mature and grow, they learn to manage their impulses while developing the ego and superego.

Secondly, Freud's theory of psychosexual development is fundamental to understanding human growth and development. According to Freud, an individual (regardless of gender) goes through five stages: oral, anal, phallic, latency, and genital. All contribute to the development of sexual and emotional drives.

It all begins with the oral stage, and the genital stage is the last to be completed. As children go through these stages of development, their needs and demands change significantly. During the oral stage, babies' behavior is more focused on feeding and dependence. In the anal stage (two to three years old), toilet training becomes the dominant concern. During the phallic stage (three to six years old), children develop an interest in their bodies, particularly their genitals, and this is where the Oedipus and Electra complexes occur. Additionally, the latency stage occurs from age seven until puberty, when sexual impulses are suppressed in order to gain knowledge, while the genital stage begins at the onset of puberty and focuses more on cultural orientation to enrich relationships.

Thirdly, Freud's psychosexual development model showed that these stages pose several challenges for human conditioning in controlling behavioral and personality traits. The crisis of each stage must be overcome in order to advance to the next level. However, unresolved conflicts or failed resolutions at any stage can create relationship challenges and other psychological problems.

From a counseling perspective, it is vital to be aware of the influence these developmental stages have on a person's psyche. We must know, for example, that according to Sigmund Freud, trauma can have profound effects on an individual's psychology. The expert argued that these traumas can cause lasting psychological damage in people and often manifest themselves in the form of emotional and mental disorders.

Freud believed that trauma can be especially harmful in childhood, as it can affect a child's emotional and cognitive development. Trauma can also have a cumulative effect, meaning that it can increase in intensity over time and have more serious effects on an individual's psychology as they age. In addition, trauma can be repressed into the unconscious, meaning that the individual may not be aware of its conscious existence. According to Freud, these repressed memories can manifest themselves in the form of mental and emotional symptoms, such as anxiety, depression, phobias, or personality disorders.

As counselors, awareness of these milestones in an individual's existence helps to unravel personality tendencies, as well as the dynamics of relationships in the normative, clinical, and forensic psychological structure.

Fourth, Freud's psychoanalytic approach emphasizes the importance of exploring unconscious thoughts, feelings, and motives in order to heal a person's mental anguish. Unconscious denial, repression, and fear of knowledge lead to mental conflict and difficulty maintaining personal balance. Conversely, becoming aware of these "unconscious" motivators and resolving them through the therapy process allows us to gain self-knowledge and acceptance.

As a therapeutic practice, psychoanalysis aims to illuminate the distortion of internal conflicts, therefore subliminally scrutinizing unconscious biases or perceptions. This process according to Freud releases primitive evolutionary conflicts while increasing awareness, triggering greater emotional regulation, which detonates stress, fantasies, and defense mechanisms.

These may include certain forms of repression, identification, rationalization, response patterns, projection, displacement, annulment, isolation, sublimation, and denial. Individuals use defense mechanisms to protect themselves from thoughts or feelings that cause them anxiety or internal conflict. They are usually unconscious reactions to conscious impulses. Feelings, for example, may be repressed or rationalized throughout life to mask stressors. The use of defense mechanisms can, however, become pathological when they are a constant substitute for dealing with real problems of stress or anxiety with which the individual is unable to cope.

Subsequently, Anna Freud, the psychoanalyst's wife, investigated five main mechanisms: repression, regression, projection, response patterns, and sublimation. Other scholars have categorized or extended the mechanisms to specific pathologies or mental health conditions. Dr. George Vaillant, for example, classified ten on a continuum of: pathological, immature, neurotic, and mature. A counselor would do well to understand defense mechanisms as a practical tool for understanding human behavior.

More specifically, defense mechanisms are psychological strategies that the ego (the conscious and rational part of the mind) uses to protect itself from anxieties and emotional tensions. Freud argued that children also use defense mechanisms in a similar way to adults and identified several defense mechanisms that children may use, including:

- **Denial:** Children may deny the reality of a situation that causes them anxiety, for example, denying that their parents are divorcing.

- **Repression**: Children may repress memories of traumatic or painful experiences to avoid feeling the associated anxiety.

- **Projection**: Children may attribute their own unacceptable feelings or thoughts to other people, for example, blaming a friend for breaking an object when it was actually the child who did it.

- **Regression:** Children may revert to childish or primitive behavior, such as thumb sucking or bedwetting, when under stress or anxiety.

- **Reactive formation:** Children may act in a manner contrary to their true feelings to avoid anxiety or emotional conflict, such as acting affectionate toward someone they actually hate.

The use of these and other defense mechanisms is a natural and necessary way to protect oneself from anxiety and emotional stress, but they can also be harmful if used excessively or inappropriately.

Adolescents also use defense mechanisms to protect themselves from emotional distress. Freud argued that adolescence is a particularly difficult stage of emotional development. Young people may experience a great deal of anxiety and internal conflict as they face the challenges of transitioning into adulthood. Some of the defense mechanisms that adolescents may use include:

- **Denial:** Teens might deny the reality of a situation that makes them anxious, like saying they don't have a drug or alcohol problem.

- **Repression:** adolescents may repress memories of traumatic or painful experiences to avoid feeling the associated anxiety.

- **Projection:** adolescents may project the problems they experience at home onto other environments, such as school, and vent their anger on teachers, classmates, etc., even if they have nothing to do with the situation.

- **Idealization**: adolescents may idealize other people or situations to avoid facing reality. For example, they may idealize a romantic partner as "the perfect person," an artist, or a television series to escape the pain they feel.

- **Sublimation:** adolescents may channel their unacceptable impulses or desires into socially acceptable activities, such as sports or art.

Adults also use defense mechanisms to protect themselves from anxiety and emotional stress, as all individuals use them to some extent as a normal part of human psychology. Some of the defense mechanisms that adults may use include:

- **Repression:** Adults may also repress memories of traumatic or painful experiences to avoid feeling the associated anxiety.

- **Denial:** Adults may deny the reality of a situation that causes them anxiety, for example, denying that they have a serious illness or marital problems, believing that this will make the problem go away.

- **Projection:** Adults may attribute their own unacceptable feelings or thoughts to other people, for example, blaming a coworker for lack of productivity when in reality it is their own lack of motivation that is causing the problem.

- **Rationalization:** Adults may justify their behavior or decisions to avoid anxiety, for example, justifying an expensive purchase by saying it is a necessary investment.

- **Sublimation:** Adults may channel their unacceptable impulses or desires into socially acceptable activities, such as work or volunteering. For example, an adult who has aggressive impulses may channel them into physical activities, such as boxing or weightlifting, rather than acting violently toward other people. In this case, the adult is using sublimation in a healthy way to channel their aggressive impulses into a socially acceptable activity that is beneficial to their physical and mental health.

Finally, Freudian theories of human growth and development have a profound influence on a counselor's practice techniques, providing them with different intervention models designed for specific effectiveness. One example is narrative therapy, developed as an application of postmodern therapies based on the notion that reality and truth are generated through storytelling. Clients are encouraged to create their own versions of subjective experiences so that, when confronted with a "conflict" in the context of psychoanalytic study, the client recognizes discrepancies for further reflection.

In conclusion, it is essential to approach the Freudian system of psychoanalytic theories with due care while affirming the fundamental principles that can be of great benefit in both counseling and psychotherapy practices. The idea of the id, ego, and superego can clarify the origin and nature of an individual's psychological problems.

The psychoanalytic therapeutic approach allows for understanding and diagnosis, thereby comprehending the unconscious motivational forces responsible for the logic and behavior of the individual. Furthermore, the application of the notion of anti-sexism for example can help break down the stereotypes that prevail in the therapy environment and the respective therapeutic setting. The application of examples of Freudian schemes strengthens the clinical aspects and the broad-ranging fundamental or theoretical principles of the field of therapy. The application of examples of Freudian schemas can strengthens the clinical aspects and the fundamental or theoretical principles of the broad domain of therapy.

EXERCISE ON FREUD'S PSYCHIC APPARATUS

The id

- Represents uncoordinated instinctive tendencies.
- Constitutes basic drives and human behavior.
- Contains our primitive desires for gratification.
- Pleasure principle.

The ego

- It represents the organized side.
- It also represents the realistic side.

The superego

- Represents the ethical role.
- Also represents the moralistic role.
- Counteracts the ego.

Reflections:

- What effect does trauma have on the biological development of a child according to Freud?
- What effect does the role of parents have on the biological development of a child according to Freud?

EXERCISE ON HUMAN DEVELOPMENT BASED ON SEXUALITY

Oral phase

- Newborns.
- During breastfeeding.

Anal phase

- Infantile pleasure.
- Control of the sphincter muscles.

Phallic phase

- Children notice parents of the opposite sex.
- Develops a coping model.
- Control of gratification.

Latency period

- Development of psychic strength.
- Inhibiting sexual impulses.
- Reducing direction.

Genital phase

- During adolescence with the maturation of the organs.

Sexual phase

- Surge of desire and sexual impulse.

Reflections

- What effect does the development of sexual identity have on an adolescent according to Freud's theories?

EXERCISE ON THE DEVELOPMENT OF DEFENSE MECHANISMS

Level 1: Pathological

- Psychotic denial.
- Delusional projection.

Level 2: Immature

- Fantasy and projection.
- Passive aggression.
- Acting out.

Level 3: Neurotic

- Intellectualization.
- Reactive formation.

- Dissociation.
- Displacement.
- Repression.

Level 4: Mature

- Humor and sublimation.
- Suppression and altruism.
- Anticipation.

Reflections:

- How do children, adolescents, and adults use defense mechanisms to justify their wrong actions or thoughts? Name a few.

_____

_____

Alfred Adler's social development theory.

Alfred Adler, a Viennese psychiatrist and founder of individual psychology, proposed a theory of human growth and development that offered an alternative to the Freudian psychoanalytic approach. Adler's theory emphasizes interpersonal relationships and the subjective experience of reality and individual growth. This section will examine Adler's fundamental principles, as we did with Freud, and explore how significant they are in counseling and psychotherapy. Let's take a look.

First, Adler's theory of human growth and development focuses on the concept of the struggle for superiority. Adler believed that individuals are driven by the need to overcome inferiority and become competent and worthy members of society. He proposed that people experience feelings of inferiority due to physical, social, and cultural differences that stimulate them to adopt behavioral and personal changes aimed at reducing those gaps. He suggested that feelings of inferiority can motivate adaptive or destructive behavior, mainly due to perceived expectations. Therefore, a sense of encouragement and self-meaning is achieved when personal idealism is recognized and complemented by individual experience.

Secondly, Adler's philosophy of holistic personal development is based on his approach called individual psychology, which delves into various elements that make up an individual's personality. Adler's theories reinforce the importance of considering various domains of life, in addition to internal motivation or personality neurosis. These include the examination of objective reality, such as sociocultural factors and personal goals, and subjective reality, such as individual perspectives, emotions, and thoughts, which emerge from a combination of experiences throughout an extensive life span, affecting the perception of individual goals or purposes.

Thirdly, Adler's concept of social embedding reinforces the emphasis on the individual's interpersonal connections with their social-relational environment. Personal development, according to individual psychology, ideally balances self-interest and empathy, as these are two critical life experiences that enable someone to navigate personal perfection and interpersonal competence.

Within psychotherapy processes, this information provides useful foundations for counselors to engage in introspection in order to understand the impact of social status or context on the configuration of an individual's personal goals, while improving the influence of egocentric cognitions. Therefore, promoting social competence by counseling people is achieved by establishing a balance between their private goals and interpersonal relationships in defining their reality.

Fourth, Alfred Adler's theory identifies the influence of parents in the formation of an individual's personality and growth as fundamental. It suggests that the dynamics of the parent-child relationship significantly influence the development of children's self-esteem, personal aspirations, and social behavior.

Adler introduced the concept of birth order and its impact on personality development. The idea is that different positions in the birth order result in different roles within the family, and interactions between siblings affect cognitive development patterns that reside within the individual psyche until adulthood. Therefore, emphasizing parental guidance and implementing an effective parenting strategy is crucial, especially to prevent personal dysfunction, the onset of anxiety, and an increase in clinical symptoms related to birth order.

Finally, Adler's emphasis on the artistic elements of individual growth contextualizes the notion of creative living. It involves setting individual goals and objectives, given one's personal appreciation of aesthetics or association with artistic expression.

Patients, through artistic expression, develop expressive anecdotes as discrete parts of individual characteristics, as well as developing therapeutic aptitude.

The therapeutic process draws psychological inferences from the individual's creative expression. By appreciating the influence of such ingenious activity, parameters can generate therapeutic modalities to address maladaptive behavior from its onset.

Adler's approach to human psychology has made valuable contributions within the connection of counseling and psychotherapy; it recognizes and acknowledges the intricate interaction of the domains of cultural and social life and their roles in the formation of subjective interpretations of reality; it balances individual goals and relational contexts and forms critical synergies for personal development and the growth of social competence.

The emphasis on social integration, birth order, and creative life are fundamental to understanding the unique narrative of the individual. Therefore, understanding Adler's theories and implementing effective intervention strategies allows for a holistic understanding of the patient's background and intentions while facilitating the exploration of personal conflicts and maladaptive behaviors that can arise.

EXERCISE ON THE INDIVIDUAL PSYCHOLOGY OF ALFRED ADLER

Teleology[1]

- Unconscious self-ideal.

- Conceals feelings of inferiority toward superiority.

- Based on social and ethical demands.

Psychodynamic system

- Study the past to alter the future.
- Integrate into the community.
- Applications here and now.

Holism

- Spiritual holism.
- Integration into larger groups.
- Religion is an example.

Reflections:

- What effect does trauma have on the self-esteem of a child and adolescent, and how would it affect their personality and integration into a group?

_____

_____

---

1. Teleology is a philosophical perspective that holds that events and processes in nature, society, and history are driven by goals, purposes, or ends. It refers to the idea that everything has a purpose or function and that natural and social phenomena move toward a specific end or outcome. Teleology has been applied in various areas of study. For example, in biology, teleology can be seen in the idea that biological structures, such as organs and systems, have a specific function and are designed to fulfill a particular purpose. In psychology, teleology can be seen in the idea that human beings seek to achieve certain objectives or goals, and in sociology it can be applied to the idea that societies evolve toward a particular state of development.

- What effect does trauma have on a woman's self-esteem, and how would it affect her integration into a group or relationship?

___

___

EXERCISE ON ALFRED ADLER'S LIFESTYLE TREE

Part One: Define the five roots

Health and appearance:

___

Economic and social position of the family.

___

Parental attitudes:

___

Family constellation:

___

Gender roles:

___

Part Two: Lifestyle

- Attitude toward oneself.
- Attitude toward difficulties.
- Attitude toward others.
- Attitude toward the opposite sex.
- Attitude toward life.

Part Three: Life tasks

- An occupation.
- Love and sex.
- Other people.

Reflections:

- According to Adler, what effect does being disabled have on the development of attitudes toward life and love?

  _____

  _____

- According to Adler, what effect does being a pretty girl or a handsome young man have on others and on oneself?

  _____

  _____

Carl Rogers and Albert Ellis' cognitive development theory.

Carl Rogers and Albert Ellis are two well-known figures in the field of counseling and psychotherapy. Both have contributed fundamental principles for human growth and deve- lopment that have had a significant impact on counseling and psychotherapy. This section will explore the fundamental principles of Carl Rogers' person-centered approach and Albert Ellis' rational emotive behavior therapy (REBT) from a counselor's perspective.

Carl Rogers' person-centered approach is based on the belief that human beings have an innate potential that can be revealed through the right kind of interpersonal encounter. Rogers believed that the most crucial factor in human growth and development is the personal relationship with the patient. He proposed that, to achieve the desired recovery experience, the counselor should help the client build a positive relationship with themselves to access and increase their self-awareness, promote positive self-esteem, self-confidence, and improve their self-concept. Rogers referred to this positive relationship as therapeutic comfort, an environment that ensures the promotion of openness and relationship.

Rogers proposed several fundamental principles that a counselor implementing his person-centered approach should adopt. First, the counselor must be authentic and open, while offering empathy and unconditional positive regard toward the patient. The patient develops close interpersonal relationships based on empathy, while recognizing internal conflicts, which makes any therapy encounter more personalized.

Second, the therapist provides a space for self-discovery, absorbed in the patient's unique experiences, perspectives, and realities. A safe environment more effectively helps the patient express their anxiety and perception of their life. Finally, the therapist's nonjudgmental approach should aim to create a nonthreatening environment that presents patients with their personal set of coping mechanisms. These techniques allow us as counselors to identify and develop acceptance of the psychological experiences of the individuals being treated, while developing new coping mechanisms to deal with similar future values.

Albert Ellis' rational emotive behavior therapy (REBT) approaches human growth and development differently than Rogers' concepts. It suggests that people experience problems due to irrational beliefs or viewpoints, which lead to emotional conflicts. This cognitive-based therapy focuses on maladaptive beliefs and automatic thoughts that limit the patient's self-assessment to promote positive habits through events and emotions. His theory emphasizes the orientation of negative thoughts in creating healthy behavior patterns.

By facilitating the dichotomy between irrational beliefs and observed evidence, rational emotive behavior therapy (REBT) helps the patient realize the importance of weighing evidence, allowing them to modify negative thought patterns to develop more efficient problem-solving mechanisms.

This therapy suggests that changing an individual's cognitive beliefs about an event can result in emotional and behavioral changes. The principles incorporated into the REBT approach can provide guidance to counselors in their psychotherapeutic efforts, as demonstrated by its widespread application in forensic and clinical psychology.

One of the focal points in treatment is the ABC model, which breaks down the individual's belief regarding a specific adversity into three parts: a sense of adversity or stressor; beliefs that intercept thoughts about adversity and establish perspectives and cognitive outcomes that lead to emotional and behavioral changes resulting from a specific situation where irrational beliefs and the ramifications of adversity become apparent. This theoretical tool is effective, in part, because it focuses on identifying targets for reinforcing healthy belief systems applied in conjunction with other psychotherapy tools: behavioral and expressive, possibly reflective and confined.

The REBT theory uses various cognitive and behavioral learning methods to achieve its goals. One technique involves challenging an individual's irrational or addictive thoughts. By delving into confidence building, introspection-oriented exposure, low self-control means to replace implicit behavior patterns, periodic inspiration, and stress management at any point in the onset of the individual's triggers, the theory aims to comprehensively moderate automatic negative reactions during traumatic experiences. The TRAC approach has been effective in managing emotional well-being issues such as anxiety and depression, behavioral disorders and addiction, as well as marital conflicts induced by a disposition toward feelings of dissatisfaction and a perception of self-rejection.

In conclusion, the theories of Carl Rogers and Albert Ellis have made significant contributions to psychotherapy. Carl Rogers' client-centered therapy approach facilitates a unique holistic process that allows the patient to change in accordance with their personality growth.

Repetitive affirmations involving authenticity, empathy, and a nonjudgmental approach provide the necessary environment for personal growth. In contrast, TRAC does not explicitly focus on natural therapeutic relationships but emphasizes an individual's belief system in creating distinctive perceptions. Therefore, counselors may need to use TRAC toolkits to address particular growth and development by modifying the cognitive approach in relation to behavior and expressive models.

Evidence gathered from forensic, clinical, and testing programs attests that these theoretical concepts formulate fundamental principles of growth across a broad sector within the domains of therapy while generating data on effective adherence to psychotherapy, expanding beyond its limitations, activating growth particularly motivated by adult conditions, justified by contemporary social recession.

COGNITIVE BEHAVIORAL THERAPY EXERCISE

Psychotherapeutic

- Aims to solve problems.
- Deals with emotions and behaviors. Is goal oriented.
- Counseling in the here and now.
- Is brief.
- Is direct.
- Is time limited.

Treatments

- Moods.
- Anxiety.
- Personality.
- Eating.
- Medical drug use.
- Psychotic disorders.

Reflections:

Define the following important terms.

- Development:

  _____

- Couple:

  _____

- Context:

  _____

- Diversity:

  _____

Exercise

Answer, What values should a Christian Education Department in a church follow, using the divisions of cognitive human development?

Age	Stage
Prenatal Period	From conception to birth
Infancy	From birth to 18-24 months
Toddlers	From 12-15 months to 2-3 years

Early-stage classes

Childhood	From 6 to 12 years old (approximately)
Preschool	From 2 to 6 years old

Primary school classes

Adolescence	From 12 to 18 - 21 years old
Young adult	From 18 – 21 to 40 years old

Adult classes

Middle age	From 40 to 60 - 65 years old
Young adult	From 60 – 65 years old until death

Exercise

Write a paragraph about the following concepts of cognitive human development.

- Nature and nurture:
  _____

- Heredity and environment:
  _____

- Maturation and learning:
  _____

- Stages versus continuity:
  _____

- Critical periods versus sensitive periods:
  _____

- Active versus passive development:
  _____

II

COUNSELING SESSION: WHAT IT IS AND MORE

Don't judge a book by its cover," as the saying goes. When a person enters our living room or office to receive counseling, it is human nature to judge them by their behavior, appearance, or use of language, to name a few categories. However, when helping someone with mental health issues, we must allow the process to lead us to discover the real human being behind their highly developed masks and defense mechanisms. This enables the counseling process to truly get to know the person in front of you so you can support them. Getting to know them and empathizing with their pain will allow you to connect with their needs and provide the appropriate course of recovery.

A counseling session is the essence of the relationship between a person trained to listen and help find solutions to emotional problems together. The counselor prepares to guide the other person based on counseling theories and formats that facilitate the discovery of the problem and the therapies or psychological techniques that can be used to alleviate or eliminate emotional imbalances.

A counseling session generally consists of four sections:

1. Establishing the relationship.

2. Identifying the problem.

3. Taking action.

4. Ending the session.

Now, let's dive in. How do you conduct a counseling session correctly? I propose a series of steps that must be followed sequentially to ensure the best possible outcome. There is a variation that can be implemented, which I will share with you at the end of this section. Let's explain each step of the process.

Establishing the relationship

Establishing an open and trusting relationship is the foundation of any successful counseling session. It is essential that the patient feels comfortable and safe to speak honestly, openly, and freely with the counselor. An effective counseling relationship can help the patient trust the counselor and feel heard and understood, ultimately leading to a positive outcome.

The first principle in establishing an open and trusting relationship is maintaining patient confidentiality and privacy. Confidentiality and privacy mean that the counselor will keep all information shared with them within the confines of the therapy session and that the patient's personal information will not be shared with anyone without their permission. Establishing confidentiality and privacy in counseling helps create a safe space where patients can open up and experience a sense of freedom and acceptance.

Empathy is another crucial principle for building trust and openness between counselor and patient in a therapy session. The counselor should always strive to put themselves in the person's shoes, try to understand their emotions and feelings, and act accordingly. Empathy helps the counselor connect better with the patient and create a safe and secure bond.

When the counselor perceives the patient's emotions and acknowledges them, the patient feels heard and understood. As a result, they will be more open in the process and willing to collaborate for their own benefit, because they know that the person accompanying them has the sensitivity to take care of all the information they are providing, which is, let's say, almost sacred.

Another principle that establishes trust and clarity is the authenticity of the counselor. They must always be authentic, honest, transparent, and genuine in their interactions with the patient. This aspect of authenticity helps patients feel a special connection and, therefore, creates an atmosphere conducive to productive counseling sessions. When the counselor is genuine, the patient feels confident, respected, and valued, which leads to a more effective therapeutic outcome.

Finally, active listening is a central principle when it comes to establishing trust and openness in therapy. Active listening is achieved by paying attention to the patient and their needs with genuine intent, looking them in the eye, avoiding distractions from cell phones or other electronic devices, maintaining a non-judgmental attitude, and listening to what they say without judgment, assumptions, or preconceived notions.

When counselors put the patient's needs first and listen attentively, they establish a healthy relationship between themselves and the patient and create an environment in which the patient feels truly heard. Feeling heard is fundamental to the therapeutic process. The patient does not feel ignored or minimized.

In conclusion, establishing open and trusting relationships in counseling sessions begins with maintaining confidentiality and privacy. The counselor must ensure that they are genuine, empathetic, authentic, and must strive to engage in active listening during the session to ensure that the patient's needs are met.

When an atmosphere of trust, understanding, and openness is established, and the counselor maintains it, the patient feels safe, heard, respected, and valued. These actions undoubtedly bring about positive change. These fundamental principles make the patient feel comfortable and relaxed, help them share their problems and concerns freely and openly, with a sense of security in the other person, with transparency in a therapy session, and ultimately lead them to growth and real results, which is sought through counseling.

Identifying the problem

Finding the real problems or issues in a counseling session can be a difficult task for the counselor. Often, patients seek counseling because they don't know where to start or how to identify the root causes of their challenges. As counselors, it is important to use effective techniques and strategies to uncover the real difficulties affecting a patient.

The first step a counselor must take to detect or identify the real issues is to broaden the patient's perspective. The problems, usually hidden beneath the symptoms that the patient shares during the first session, may be broader or deeper and may also come from sources that have not been previously explored in the discussion. To achieve this, discussions with the patient should be conversational and exploratory, extremely careful and non-invasive, but proactive. Ask open-ended questions that allow patients to provide detailed descriptions of how they feel in order to learn about their thoughts on various topics. That is ideal at this stage.

The next step is to use probing questions. As the patient describes their experiences, the counselor should ask probing questions that challenge, clarify, or test the assumptions they present. Open-ended questions are specific in content, focused on quality, and elicit long, complex responses from the patient; they expand on areas that, if done correctly, expose the real issues. Probing questions allow the counselor to refine the patient's perspective by helping to separate possible feelings of discomfort, anxiety, or depression from the real problems.

Thirdly, the counselor should consider establishing the pattern of emotional resonances by examining how it fits with the criteria presented at the beginning. At this stage, it is necessary to analyze what triggers the patients' emotions in the present moment. From that point on, the therapist can decode the underlying struggle. As the patient speaks, the counselor should keep up with their descriptions and observe patterns and triggers that help establish and thematically segment primary, secondary, or tertiary emotions. This strategy will highlight the key factors that drive the patient's thought process, emotions, and reactions in a controlled and safe environment.

Fourth, using the technique of exploring past experiences in depth can shed light on the fundamental factors that triggered the creation and maintenance of problematic symptoms. Early childhood experiences and their resulting influences, such as damage to self-esteem or the bond with parents, can exert a powerful ongoing effect that contributes to destructive beliefs that could be the source of the patient's problems. By effectively encouraging the patient to recall past experiences and consistently asking the question "why?" until there is no further depth to explore, one can follow the thread that leads to identifying the root cause of these harmful beliefs and bringing them to consciousness.

Finally, counselors must recognize contradictory elements that could be masking underlying problems, whether due to the patient's origins or their current state. The counselor does this by promoting role-playing sessions that deeply reflect and modify the possibilities and opportunities to be attentive and tolerant when the patient shows signs of confusion, hesitation, or remorse. This strategy can lead a patient to reevaluate a problem, causing them to reassess their ideas and clarify the real problem areas.

In conclusion, finding the real problems or issues in counseling is an ongoing process that aims to resolve or improve symptom relief. It is a constantly updated process, which involves a continuous understanding of patients as they progress through sessions to discover the root of problems without venturing too far from the conventional approach aimed at improving progress.

It encompasses a combination of probing questions that allow the counselor to analyze patterns and themes of emotions, in-depth exploration of past experiences, confrontation and evaluation of discrepancies and problematic beliefs to discover how to bring them to light with empathy. In this way, patients are more likely to gain insight into the areas that cause them distress and learn how to move past their problems.

Taking action

The counselor can use various techniques to help. Christian counselors, in particular, can use guided prayer and draw on mentors or support groups to follow up with a person as appropriate. However, I recommend that the basis of counseling focus on the bibliotherapy. In the next section, I will expand on the use of bibliotherapy as a separate strategy to this counseling model.

Bibliotherapy is a useful tool for counselors to integrate into therapy sessions. Bibliotherapy can be described as the use of literature and reading in the context of mental health and well-being. It can be divided into three categories, including self-help, motivational, and guidance books, as well as fiction and nonfiction books that offer psychological theories and research findings. Literally interpreted as "book therapy," bibliotherapy is an evidence-based therapeutic approach used to treat a wide range of psychological and emotional problems. It helps patients find solutions, new insights, and perspectives for their problems in a controlled environment that extends beyond the therapy period.

There are several factors that a counselor must consider when selecting appropriate bibliotherapy options for patients. Here are four.

The first factors that the counselor must consider are the problems or issues presented by the patient. For a set of books to be effective in counseling, it must directly match the patient's problems. The counselor must be thoughtful, choosing books that are relevant, credible, informative, and specific to the patient's difficulties and experiences. For example, if the patient has trouble sleeping, the counselor should select books that offer coping mechanisms that reflect sleep hygiene, as well as other related topics that could cause anxiety and stress, such as insomnia due to different workloads, PTSD, among others.

Second, the counselor must consider the context of the patient's treatment. The process of selecting texts within bibliotherapy depends largely on the stage of a patient's treatment.

When deciding which books to recommend to patients, the counselor should choose those that reflect the patient's stage of development. For example, people in the early stages of recovery may benefit most from books about acceptance and preparing for the new journey ahead, while those in a later stage of recovery may need books about finding hope and adopting new perspectives.

The third factor to consider is clinical relevance to the patient's culture. The counselor should take time to choose material that is consistent with the patient's cultural background. For example, when working with patients from different cultures, the counselor should consider whether the selected literature fits with their cultural values, customs, and ideals, and whether it avoids perpetuating stereotypes and offensive language based on racial or ethnic nuances.

The fourth and final factor corrects the information or theory when choosing the group of texts to carry out bibliotherapy. Counselors should choose books that are based on current research and officially recognized therapeutic theories to verify the reliability of their content. As such, patients receive authentic information and insights into how problems might affect them throughout their lives. Counselors must have sufficient background and training on which theories or interventions are beneficial and which categories are most acceptable for particular situations.

In conclusion, bibliotherapy in modern counseling can be of great value to both counselors and patients to achieve faster changes in their behavior and in post-therapy environment. Knowing which selection is most appropriate in bibliotherapy is essential to improving the outcome of sessions. By analyzing the presentation of patients' problems and issues, factors that may arise within the context, cultural differences, and consistency with existing treatments and modern therapies, counselors can select quality literature that could be used successfully to achieve patients' self-discovery and build a solid foundation for a deep therapeutic relationship. When these factors are taken seriously, the counselor is more likely to choose literature that has proven effective in addressing patients' problems, integrating them, and thus maintaining progress.

Ending the counseling session

Ending counseling sessions is one of the most challenging and delicate parts of counseling therapy. When counseling sessions are coming to an end, counselors generally experience feelings of accomplishment, but they may also experience some anxiety or uncertainty about ending the therapeutic relationship or not knowing what will happen next without the counselor's support.

Ending the counseling session can help patients move forward with their lives by equipping them with the tools necessary to manage recurring thoughts, feelings, and behaviors that could trigger an adverse mental reaction. Therefore, it is necessary for the counselor to determine how and when to end the counseling therapy session appropriately.

The first thing a counselor should consider when ending counseling sessions is whether the patient and therapist have achieved the goals that were initially set. The counselor should regularly monitor the patient's progress and assess when the objectives have been met.

The therapeutic goal sets the standard for when it is most appropriate to end the session. If both the counselor's and patient's goal setting has gone according to plan, and the patient is already practicing the coping mechanisms learned in subsequent consultations, then it is time to end the sessions since the goals have been achieved.

The second factor to consider is the patient's readiness to end the sessions. Counseling sessions should end only when the client expresses satisfaction with the progress made toward their goals and feels that they better understand their problems and have found alternative coping techniques that they could apply indefinitely beyond the counseling period. Since patients may have difficulty recognizing their readiness for counseling termination, reflecting on and identifying indicators of progress with the patient may lead to better affirmation of underlying goals.

Third, the counselor needs to determine the potential dependency that exists between patients and the therapist, whether the patient will require ongoing unconscious guidance for a period of time or will face feelings of abandonment and distress once the sessions end. Counselors can use the final counseling sessions to build a discharge plan that builds confidence and provides stability during the patient's transition. A discharge plan that includes specific activities in which the patient could participate, post-therapy planning, and how they will manage when they are activated after the session are typical components of such a plan.

Fourth, potential opportunities for additional sessions or ongoing care should be explored, such as couples therapy, group support, or other specialized therapies that may be appropriate for the patient's needs. Emotional problems may now manifest themselves during specific peak moments in the patient's life journey, as well as other challenges. Having the support of specialists or resources available to refer patients when and as needed serves as an effective buffer for managing these emergencies, as not all problems can be nipped in the bud.

Finally, the counselor must ensure that the patient's priorities and disposition do not change along with the established goals. A patient may have firmly believed that the problem presents itself consistently and work with the counselor's knowledge of the issue, but after seeing a different perspective, the patient may have a different view and then need to instill another method to correct it. It is up to the counselor to ensure that their patients have various means of receiving alternative guidance or counseling in such a scenario, provided they prefer a significant adjustment.

In conclusion, the goal of ending counseling is to enable the patient to lead a more productive and meaningful life without necessarily relying on professional intervention, while the decision to end counseling sessions may be dictated by the counselor's progress assessments as well as the independence expressed by the patient. The willingness to end the intervention and their emotional stability to move forward could result in the duration of the counseling session increasing from its initial period.

By adequately measuring the progress of counseling sessions through mutual goals, timely discharge plans that take into account aftercare options for patients in transition, which adequately empower patients to handle future situations, counselors can determine when and how to end counseling sessions.

Counseling sessions can equip patients with better life skills that increase their emotional well-being and effectively manage mental health symptoms, allowing them to create meaningful reflections for their future.

Bibliotherapy as a stand-alone format

Bibliotherapy is guided by the resources used rather than by classic counseling techniques. Bibliotherapy is another option that counselors can use outside of the previous format. It includes specific techniques and exercises. The principles of both sections can be used in combination or independently. Bibliotherapy is a well-known therapeutic approach that uses literature or books to seek solutions, provide information, solve problems, and navigate through emotional and psychological trauma. This section provides information on the steps necessary to prepare for effective bibliotherapy sessions from a counselor's perspective. Let's take a look.

Step 1: Identifying the patient's primary concerns

The counselor's primary goal is to help the patient understand their concerns. This understanding may include identifying and describing the specific problematic thoughts, feelings, and behaviors that have brought the patient to counseling. The counselor could achieve this by holding open conversations with each patient in which they are encouraged to give detailed information about their problems and what makes them feel vulnerable in order to work on categorizing the patient's problems.

Step 2: Determining session objectives

After identifying the patient's main concerns, the counselor should establish the objectives of the session and guide the patient toward a clear understanding of what they want to achieve with therapy. These objectives will guide the choice of books that focus on the specific problems raised by the patient in order to provide better angles for getting to the root of the problem. The counselor should set realistic and measurable outcomes so that both the patient and the therapist can evaluate the effectiveness of the interventions carried out by keeping track of how to easily formulate the means to overcome the crisis outlined. Generally, the materials used help the counselor determine the desired outcomes.

Step 3: Conducting Research

For effective bibliotherapy sessions, the counselor must conduct thorough research on literature and reading materials relevant to the patient's needs that also align with the previously established goals. Such sessions require complex knowledge, provided by informed sources, that offers solutions to everyday psychological disorders. Therefore, researching the required materials requires selecting materials that satisfy factors such as academic credibility, relevance, readability, and the potential effect of influencing the patient's biases or reshaping their perceptions of certain ideologies.

Step 4: Reading and examining all identified materials

The counselor should read and evaluate all materials identified through their research. When identifying appropriate material, they should make notes to facilitate discussions during the consultation and include their own observations and notes. The evaluation process separates credible materials from those that do not fit the research and objectives, such as relevance, scope of coverage, complex issues that patients need to understand, language barriers, among other issues. This step ensures quality, as what is presented can affect patient understanding and identifies to some extent what needs to be revisited, thereby providing additional information.

Step 5: Assessing biases and opinions and identifying potential triggers

The counselor must constantly assess how their opinions affect the firm foundation to determine their relevance in the therapy process. Therapists must take special care when choosing literature that could trigger potentially harmful actions for the patient.

A therapist's bias regarding the patient's problems can make the intervention less effective than usual. Therefore, the literature should be predominantly aligned with the patient's mindset, or the patient may become defensive and less likely to engage or recognize the daily implications of their harmful actions toward others. It is the counselor's responsibility to raise this issue with compassion and empathy that evokes openness so that emotions are not repressed but analyzed.

Step 6: Setting the stage, provide a safe learning environment, perception

The patient's experience during bibliotherapy sessions should be structured as a guided discovery, an exploration of self-realization. Demonstrating a non-intrusive environment that facilitates patient participation in discussions provides comfort in expressing the unique problems they face. Not everything related to bibliotherapy should be strictly conducted through records. By creating a reference point to the concept, patients who are convinced they will reach their desired destination add value to bibliotherapy sessions.

Step 7: Providing guidance and homework

At the end of each session, the counselor should provide guidance to help the patient get the most value from the literature that was presented or read during the session. This will be enhanced by various assignments, such as self-reflection journals, in which the patient is asked to evaluate and describe how the literature presented or read helps them better understand their feelings and anxieties while allowing them to identify fragile ground and triggers from a non-judgmental perspective. They could also be encouraged to try exercises that further develop their overall pursuit of mental health enlightenment through bibliotherapy books in different categories that will be provided by the counselor.

Step 8: Ongoing sessions and referrals

Finally, for bibliotherapy sessions to be carried out efficiently, the counselor must evaluate the patient's progress as they participate in these sessions on an ongoing basis. For those who require additional support, information will be provided on support options beyond counseling sessions, such as referrals to group support structures for those who need similar teams to rebuild their thought processes and other specialized therapy groups that align with their particular problem, e.g., PTSD or addictions.

In conclusion, when preparing for bibliotherapy sessions, from a counselor's perspective, it is of great importance to identify the patient's main concerns, research, read, and evaluate materials, identify biases and opinions, establish a conducive environment, provide guidance and assignments, and continuously evaluate patients' progress.

The refined masterpiece is created from the curriculum established in the initial phases, which evaluate key aspects before, during, and after counseling sessions. The guideline, of course, means that the patient feels understood, respected, and guided at every step of the journey and with a strong sense of belonging. With well-designed bibliotherapy sessions with every measure and point in place, healing can thrive beyond longer periods of therapy, and people will find a new appreciation for the subtle academic material that offers a component of self-exploration.

Classic counseling model	Bibliotherapy model
<ul><li>Establish a relationship</li><li>Identify the problem</li><li>Take action</li><li>End sessions</li></ul>	<ul><li>Identifying patient concerns</li><li>Setting session goals</li><li>Conducting research (searching for books or articles for counseling sessions)</li><li>Reading and critiquing all identified materials</li><li>Assessing biases</li><li>Setting the stage, facilitating a safe learning environment: perception</li><li>Providing guidance and homework</li><li>Ongoing sessions and referrals</li></ul>

Reflections:

What do you consider to be the advantages or disadvantages of the classic model?

_____

_____

In your opinion, what do you think are the advantages or disadvantages of the bibliotherapy model?

_____

_____

Classic counseling model with an emphasis on bibliotherapy

What I recommend is a fusion of classic counseling with an emphasis on bibliotherapy. This can be done in six sessions:

Session	Action
1.	Establish relationship
2.	Bibliotherapy 1
3.	Bibliotherapy 2
4.	Bibliotherapy 3
5.	Bibliotherapy 4
6.	End sessions

References: mentors, support groups, therapy groups, etc.

Reflections:
Divide a book into four counseling sessions.

Book: _____

Session 1: _____

Session 2: _____

Session 3: _____

Session 4: _____

III.

CREATION OF COMMUNITY COUNSELING CENTERS WITH CHRISTIAN VALUES

The state of Tabasco, in southeastern Mexico, consistently has very high suicide rates. Pastors and directors of social agencies invited me to establish community counseling centers to be part of the solution to this troubling problem. From there, the idea was born to establish a community counseling center with Christian values that can serve as a beacon of hope and healing for people struggling with mental health issues by incorporating Christian principles into evidence-based practices.

To this end, we set out to help combat suicide in the state of Tabasco and be a bridge between the faith community and professional and state mental health agencies. We trained church volunteers in the logistics of establishing a clinic, although church structures are already predisposed to this type of operation. I believe that faith communities can have a significant impact on combating any mental health issue by serving as a bridge between the population and professional and government agencies.

Now, let's get down to business. In today's rapidly changing world, mental health issues have become prevalent and difficult to address in our society. As believers, we have a unique opportunity to provide comfort, support, and guidance to those in need. Establishing a community counseling center that embraces Christian values can serve as a transformative platform for providing holistic care to people struggling with such issues, which are a huge cause for concern. These local counseling centers can have a real impact when they utilize the resources available in churches, social agencies, and government entities.

The first section of this chapter explores the steps necessary to establish a community counseling center in your area. The second section provides clear ideas for building the structure of an online community counseling center.

In particular, I am hopeful that churches will be able to participate in these kinds of far-reaching and much-appreciated actions, given the facilities they have and the highly trained professionals they already employ. If a local religious community commits to helping mental health patients in this area of need, they can make a dramatic and substantial difference in the lives of families and disintegrated people.

First, it is important for the entity to decide how it will present itself to the community. A Christian-based organization must be honest and direct. It must establish a credible and relevant Christian perspective by transparently presenting its religious beliefs along with treatment options, while allowing individuals to decide whether they want to receive support from a faith-based organization.

Personally, I have often had the opportunity to help people with whom I have moral and religious differences. In fact, I consider it a Christian privilege to extend my hand of support to those who do not share my faith. What I mean is that faith is not an excuse or a reason to not reach out to more people, regardless of what they believe or what they do.

Service has nothing to do with that; in fact, it does not look at the details that might distract us from our purpose. The church is not confined to the four walls of a building where everyone speaks the same language. The idea is to impact as many people as possible and reach places where there is a greater need for guidance.

Let's get practical. This section explores the essential steps for establishing a counseling center focused on integrating Christian values while demonstrating a commitment to professional ethics and diverse scientific perspectives.

1. Assessment of community needs and objectives

The first step in establishing a Christian-based community counseling center is to conduct a comprehensive assessment of community needs and goals. This assessment should consider various factors, such as demographics, mental health statistics, and existing resources. Engaging with local churches, pastors, and community leaders can provide valuable insight into prevalent issues and help determine the center's areas of focus and essential services.

2. Trained and professional staff

To cultivate a successful counseling center, it is essential to assemble a competent and compassionate workforce. It is paramount to hire accredited mental health professionals with experience in various counseling modalities.

In addition, providing training in the integration of Christian principles with evidence-based therapies will ensure that the counseling center offers effective and faith-informed care, an important element in overcoming any challenge in people's lives.

Similarly, the center must commit to ongoing supervision, continuing education, and ensuring compliance with ethical guidelines, which will help maintain high-quality services and prevent the work done in the early stages from being lost, thus gaining momentum and bearing fruit in the long term.

3. Infrastructure and resources

We often believe that the environment is not relevant or that it takes a back seat to the actions to be taken at deeper levels. However, creating a welcoming physical space is crucial to establishing a counseling center aligned with Christian values. This space should reflect human warmth, openness, and acceptance, which are basic principles of a faith-based counseling approach. The availability of technology should also be considered, such as appropriate electronic devices, telehealth services, and others that may be proposed based on the operation of online counseling, to ensure accessibility for people who may have difficulty visiting the center physically. Establishing a broad network of resources, including connections with churches, community organizations, and support groups, will provide beneficiaries with a wide range of community-based support.

4. Comprehensive Care Approach

A key aspect of a Christian-based community counseling center is the integration of spiritual and psychological dimensions into therapy or care, as a comprehensive approach. This symbiosis must address people's mental, emotional, and spiritual needs, recognizing that psychological and spiritual well-being are interconnected and impossible to separate.

Counselors must have the ability to facilitate dialogue about faith, prayer, and biblical principles, while respecting each individual's beliefs and personal background. Cultivating an environment that encourages the exploration of spirituality can help patients find meaning, purpose, and hope in their healing process.

5. Collaboration with local churches and Christian organizations

Working in collaboration with local churches and Christian organizations enhances the breadth of services provided by the counseling center, fosters a harmonious climate among all participants, and produces an interesting exchange that enriches the work. Establishing partnerships facilitates referrals, provides opportunities for spiritual growth and community integration, and promotes holistic healing. Regular communication and involvement with clergy can also ensure that counselors receive comprehensive guidance and incredible team support as they address faith-related concerns. Remember, partnerships are never a bad thing; on the contrary, "unity is strength" (in unity there is strength)

6. Cultural sensitivity and inclusion

Although a counseling center is guided by Christian values, it is essential that it adopt cultural sensitivity and a sense of inclusion with true recognition of the importance this has in any social work.

Recognizing and valuing diversity within the community, fostering an environment free of discrimination or judgment, is an action that should never be neglected in group work. Where there are people, there is diversity, and where there is diversity, there is richness. Therefore, counseling centers must always practice sufficient humility to tolerate, accept, and be flexible to what is new and different. Likewise, training on cultural traits and the development of awareness and understanding of diverse cultural backgrounds and religious traditions should be promoted.

A community counseling center must ensure that each patient receives care while respecting their particular experience.

Ultimately, establishing a Christian-based community counseling center can serve as a beacon of hope and healing for individuals struggling with mental health issues by incorporating Christian principles into evidence-based practices.

By providing a welcoming environment and fostering cultural sensitivity, the center can offer a holistic approach to counseling that emphasizes the unique integration of spirituality and mental health. This initiative requires a collaborative effort from the community, local churches, and mental health professionals committed to encouraging others with empathy, understanding, and faith. Together, we can create a counseling center that promotes people's well-being and nurtures them, while strengthening the community, guided by the teachings of Christ and the principles of professional counseling.

Creating Virtual Counseling Centers with Christian Values

As the world continues to transform with technological advances, online platforms have become essential for connecting people and providing services. In the field of mental health, an online community counseling center with Christian values can be a powerful tool for reaching people, regardless of their geographic location.

This chapter explores the steps necessary to establish an online counseling center that integrates Christian values and ensures accessible, faith-based care for people struggling with mental health issues.

1. Develop a comprehensive and achievable plan
Implementing a detailed plan and creating clear objectives is vital to establishing an online community counseling center with Christian values. This plan should include an assessment of the target population, the services to be offered, and the role the center will play in the community. Identifying key objectives, such as providing accessible counseling services, integrating Christian principles, and cultivating a strong support network, will guide the center's vision and mission.

2. Technology and Platform Selection
Choosing the right technology and platforms is crucial to the success of an online counseling center. Consider factors such as ease of use, security, and HIPAA (Health Insurance Portability and Accountability Act) compliance to ensure the privacy and confidentiality of client information. I recommend using video conferencing software, secure messaging platforms, and online counseling platforms that facilitate real-time interactions and provide a reliable, seamless experience.

3. Recruiting and training counselors
Assembling a team of qualified and compassionate counselors is vital to the success of an online counseling center. It is important to recruit accredited counselors who are comfortable providing virtual counseling and who possess the necessary technological skills. On the other hand, comprehensive training must be offered to new counselors on an ongoing basis, ensuring that they have a solid understanding of Christian values and know how to effectively integrate them into the counseling process. Fostering a supportive

and collaborative environment that promotes ongoing professional development and supervision of collaborators will greatly enhance the practice of counseling in all its forms.

4. Establishing an outreach strategy

Developing an effective outreach strategy is essential for reaching people seeking counseling services in a digital environment. Leverage social media, websites, and other platforms to promote the services provided by the counseling center. Form partnerships with churches and Christian organizations, create community outreach programs to increase visibility and facilitate referrals. Participate in targeted advertising efforts to highlight the faith-based approach of the counseling center and reach those who are in harmony with this proposal.

5. Incorporate Christian principles

Infusing Christian values into the counseling process helps patients appreciate the spiritual dimension of their struggles to foster hope and resilience. Counselors must have the ability to integrate biblical principles, prayer, and spiritual practices while respecting the diversity of beliefs among the patient population. Regular staff meetings, supervision sessions, and ongoing training can help counselors deepen their understanding of Christian principles and their application in the counseling setting.

6. Focus on accessibility and inclusion

Ensuring accessibility and inclusion is crucial for an online community counseling center. To do this, use accessible technology platforms, provide multiple communication options, and consider translating materials or offering interpreters to accommodate people from diverse backgrounds. In this regard, never forget to keep the center up to date with technology and the emergence of new digital resources.

Be mindful of cultural sensitivities and highlight them as a core value of the counseling center. Maintain a commitment to respect and inclusion to foster an online environment where people feel safe and valued.

We can conclude that establishing an online Christian-based community counseling center presents a unique opportunity to reach people in need of mental health support, regardless of their geographic location.

By developing a comprehensive plan, leveraging technology, and recruiting and training qualified counselors, we can establish an online counseling center that integrates Christian principles into these evidence-based practices.

By empowering people with hope, healing, and spiritual support, this initiative reflects the essence of Christian values while offering accessible and inclusive care to those in need. Working together, we can have a lasting impact on people's mental health and well-being and foster their spiritual, emotional, and psychological growth.

IV.

Family and Counseling

The traditional nuclear couple, with their dependent children, is the basic social unit we commonly refer to as family. This is the foundation upon which all human psychology is formed, the beginning of everything. It has been a standard for models of human growth and development in history and modern psychology. That is, the heterosexual family is responsible for all human life on earth. Otherwise, it would not have been possible.

This does not mean, however, that married life is free of great challenges. Beyond the biological concerns of human sexual attraction and fertility, marriage requires legal and moral rules that protect adults and children from civil society.

In the original Hebrew the book of Genesis was called "In the beginning", and in the first chapter we are presented with a family that we have always heard about, and it is composed by Adam and Eve. According to the biblical record, from the beginning of time humans that identified as male and female were created in the image of God. Judeo-Christian values in Western civilizations have adopted the moral demands placed on human life to define our inalienable rights, and the family structure has been historically established as worthy of protection and intrinsic value.

This chapter celebrates the inherent value of marriage and teaches healthy rules for husbands and wives. At the end, it includes a section specifically on the treatment and care that should be given in counseling to a couple going through a divorce process.

The role of the father

Being a father and family man is both rewarding and challenging. It involves responsibility, sacrifice, and patience. In addition to being a successful experience, it is important to understand the principles governing the role of father and family man. From a counselor's perspective, it is essential to highlight these fundamentals to help guide and support parents and family men through difficult times.

Fundamental principles governing the role of a father and family man from the perspective of a counselor

1. Leadership and accountability
One of the fundamental principles governing the role of father and family man is leadership and responsibility. The father is the family leader and as such has a responsibility

to provide direction, values and a sense of unity. The leadership of the father is vital in setting the tone for family growth and development. In this sense, the advice of a father is to lead by example. This means being involved in the lives of your children and other family members, showing a strong work ethic, and being consistent in your behavior. By leading by example, fathers earn the respect of their family members and, in turn, listen to them and receive guidance.

2. Communication

Communication is another fundamental principle governing the role of father and family man. Counselors should warn fathers to prioritize communication in their relationships with their spouse and children. Effective communication involves actively listening while showing empathy and providing peace of mind. The father should strive to understand their children's needs, dreams and challenges and communicate openly and sincerely with them. It is important for the father to avoid preaching to your children but also listen and explain with patience and empathy.

3. Love

Love is the glue that binds families together; it is therefore the fundamental principle governing the role of father and family man. It is important that the father loves his children unconditionally for who they are. Counselors warn fathers to show not only affection but also interest in their children's lives. Love can be expressed in kind words, by sharing quality time and showing interest in the things that concern children. Fathers who show love gain the trust and respect of their children and can influence them in a positive way.

4. Consistency and discipline

Consistency and discipline are crucial to a child's development. Counselors warn fathers to set clear boundaries and expectations for their children and to comply with them consistently. Although it can be a challenge for fathers to provide discipline, both in rewards and restrictions, it is important for their children's development. Communicating is expected of children with respect to behavior that helps set clear boundaries. Where appropriate, they should administer discipline to help correct negative behavior or reinforce positive behavior in children.

5. Model to follow

Fathers play a vital role as role models in their children's lives. Counselors urge fathers to show positive behaviors and habits that their children can model. For example, a father who values education and lifelong learning sets a good example by continuing to grow, including encouraging your children to practice good study habits. A father who practices empathy toward others demonstrates mutual respect and promotes the development of good manners.

In conclusion, as a father and family man his role is not easy but very gratifying. The principles governing this role are crucial and, although most fathers aspire to implement them routinely, they can be difficult to maintain. By adopting the principles of leadership and responsibility, communication, love, consistency, discipline and role model from a counselor's perspective, fathers can lead successful lives with healthy and productive families.

The role of a mother

Being a mother and family woman is a challenging task that involves great responsibility and sacrifice. It can also be an immensely satisfying experience, both on a personal and interpersonal level. The role of a mother and a family woman requires a good understanding of the essential principles that guide them. A counselor can help mothers understand these guiding fundamentals. In this section we will explore the foundations governing the role of a mother and a family woman from the perspective of a counselor.

Fundamental principles governing the role of a mother and a family woman from the perspective of a counselor

1. Parenting and compassion

One of the fundamental principles guiding the role of a mother and a family woman is parenting and compassion. Mothers have a natural instinct to create a safe, warm and welcoming environment for your children. From the counselors' perspective, it is essential to recognize and encourage this instinct to support mothers in raising emotionally resilient children. Compassion is equally important, as it allows for unconditional love and tolerance when supporting family members. By showing compassion, a mother brings her family together and creates healthy relationships that can be harnessed in difficult times.

2. Communication

Effective communication is crucial to promoting healthy family relationships. Mothers must actively listen, support and provide guidance to their children and family members. They also naturally have this ability. From the counselors' point of view, effective communication also includes encouraging open communication by reserving quality time, time to discuss feelings, as well as setting the table, with love and understanding, concerns and problems that may arise for others. Finally, the mother must properly explain the whys and the wherefores of each action requested, required or suggested so that the children understand that it is not by whim, but because each command, order and recommendation conceals the development of great skills that the family needs for life.

3. Empathy and emotional intelligence

Mothers can strongly influence the emotional intelligence of their children by showing empathy. Empathy is the ability to understand others' feelings and perspectives based on their experiences.

From the counselors' point of view, fostering emotional intelligence is fundamental to proper socialization and transcending family problems. Mothers should model and teach their children empathy at an early age, creating healthy and noble behaviors for life.

By relating to others, the mother shows her children how to understand and accept differences while developing skills for interaction, which improves family relationships.

4. Personal care

Counselors suggest that it is important for mothers to set aside some time to take care of themselves, stressing that they should not feel guilty when they are allowed to: go out with their girlfriends, have dinner with the husband without the children, go to the cinema, the beauty salon, to paint, to do sport or simply to indulge. It is impossible for a mother to give of herself if she is exhausted or worn out from taking care of others. Personal care allows a mother to relocate, mentally relax and regain energy to carry on with her responsibilities. Women can better relate to their role as mothers from the joy of caring for themselves. This is a fundamental principle as critical, but sometimes ignored for moms. Parenting in the hands of a tired mother is less effective than in the hands of a mother who puts herself first. A woman who does what she likes, who is self-confident, who has not been neglected since being a mother and who is constantly seeking to grow has much to teach her children with her behavior, emotional independence, self-respect, freedom to choose the life you want, and tenacity.

5. Consistency and discipline

Consistency and discipline are considered essential principles governing the role of mother and wife in the family. A woman who teaches discipline on an ongoing basis helps her children create good habits, which impact positive family interactions as a whole. When moms offer consistent responses to their children, they feel that they have an environment that cares for them, shows understanding of what adults hope to do, and maintain healthy family habits and connections. Discipline has a positive influence on their self-esteem and personal responsibility. They see it not as a punishment, but as an adequate way of guarding themselves from certain things in life from which they can be freed or come out unscathed only through the discipline that has been instilled in them.

6. Understanding the importance of playing

While mothers focus on their caregiving responsibilities, it can be easy for them to get caught up in routines and schedules. Counselors suggest that it is important for mothers to set aside time to play with their children. Play serves a vital role in family routines to create bonds and develop healthy socializing habits. By engaging in play with their children in various settings, mothers also gain experiences of mental, physical, emotional and social growth. Without sacrificing daily routine, play, leisure and recreation, the moments of relationship are part of the balance that in life creates stability and family union.

Finally, we can say that being a mother and wife brings with it immense responsibilities and can be both stressful and rewarding. Counselors can provide valuable support by guiding women on the fundamental principles governing their role in the family structure.

Principles governing the role of mother and wife include parenting and compassion, communication, empathy and emotional intelligence, personal care, constancy, discipline and enjoyable gaming experiences. The counselors' view is that by implementing these principles, mothers can achieve a balanced family life with optimal growth and happiness.

Benefits of a family with both parents

Raising children is no small matter and requires a lot of effort and resources. When it comes to parenting, there are different family structures. Some children are raised by single parents, grandparents or other family members. However, there are significant advantages to raising children in a family with both parents. From a counselor's perspective, these benefits have a substantial impact on the child's long-term well-being and success. This chapter will delve into the benefits of raising children in a mother and father family, from the perspective of a counselor.

Advantages of raising children in a family with both parents

1. Financial stability
One of the most significant benefits of raising children in a family with both parents is that more economic resources are provided. Two-parent families tend to have more stability and financial security than one-parent families. With both parents involved in the economic contribution there is more financial security for the family. Financial stress can lead to psychological problems in children, and a family with both parents removes some of that financial burden, which reduces this type of stress and promotes emotional well-being.

2. Sets the model to follow
In the family of both parents, both the figure of the mother and the father are present in the child's life, and this can provide a balanced perspective on life. Father and mother provide different parenting styles that add value as they fit their typical characters, where the mom is tender and loving and the dad is powerful and full of guidance. As a result, children are exposed to different approaches, opinions and solutions when trying to solve problems. Witnessing the role model of both mom and dad gives them an important opportunity to promote healthy, balanced socialization.

3. Autonomy and academic success
Research suggests that children raised in families with both parents are more likely to enjoy higher levels of academic success and perceived support and love. Positive family support improves learning, independence, emotional intelligence and resilience to overcome the obstacles they face. In most cases, families with both parents provide enough emotional and psychological support to build stability, self-esteem and confidence for better academic success.

4. Longer support provision
While everyone becomes an adult and sometimes leaves home to focus on their career and personal life, staying in a home with both parents provides more support from the

same loving people. With parents who love and respect each other by communicating and working together, adult children can benefit in their own life plans. Important decisions are made when mothers and fathers provide professionalism, and positive support to improve mental well-being.

5. Physical and emotional security

Children need physical and emotional security, and both parents are important in providing that sense of security. Emotional and physical security leads to happy moments and proper mental health for children. Although the two types of security offer care and are different, a home with both parents ensures an automatic level of stability for children through affirmation words for a long and unpredictable future. Children raised in two-parent homes feel this collective support, especially in a world full of any kind of uncertainty.

In conclusion, a biparental family oversees the task of raising their child with different developmental perspectives that avoid dissatisfaction and exhaustion. Raising a child in a family with both parents guarantees some benefits: physical and emotional security, the kind of autonomy that leads to academic success (which inspires personal growth), greater financial stability, various role models and longer-term support. Of course, not all households are equal, and each family goes through its various challenges and successes, playing an important role in the cognitive and emotional well-being of each child. From a counselor's perspective, raising children in a home with both parents leaves positive marks for life.

The divorce

Divorce is a complex issue that often involves significant emotional, financial and legal challenges. Both sides lose a significant level of emotional support and awareness around various issues surrounding it, such as alienation that amplifies negative traits. Although divorce can offer a new beginning and provide much-needed relief to problems that result in marital dissatisfaction, it has a significant impact on mental health. As counselors, in addition to providing support, we need to teach that people who are getting divorced face greater challenges of emotional and psychological types: anxiety, depression, stress and sudden lifestyle changes, therefore require access to support resources during such transitions.

A critical function of divorce counselors is to provide an environment of support and empathy without judging clients seeking therapy. Part of this process is to recognize the complexity of living through these challenges, avoiding oversimplifying problems and refraining from condemning such clients.

Counselors should try to understand the experiences of clients before reaching conclusions. Encouraging and listening with attention and sensitivity provides crucial guidance for identifying solutions. Counselors must minimize the tagging of clients from the point of view of a society that both sides are undoubtedly aware of in theory, through non-violent communication skills dictated by relationship counseling techniques.

Secondly, since divorce is a unique experience that affects each person differently, counselors should use relevant and effective counseling methodologies during the therapeutic process, such as narrative counseling, focusing on solution or cognitive therapy techniques.

Using counseling techniques, clients can identify deep-rooted problems that underlie marital conflicts. By creating open behavior, genuinely listening and carefully reviewing customer perceptions reveal perspectives the long-term risk associated with typical generalized mental health predispositions.

Finally, whether advising people during a divorce process is crucial, Counselors should also provide coping strategies on how both parties can adjust to their new lives after the completion of divorce-related legal processes and beyond.

The counselor should provide clients with essential healing practices, such as stress management, knowledge of healthier approaches to communication and support systems outside of the broken relationship. The provider may be able to align clients with community programs or mental health treatments, such as counseling for inpatients and outpatients who are having difficulty making the transition.

In conclusion, divorce presents many emotional and mental health challenges that require professional care. Both sides struggle with important problems, so understanding each other's perspective and reliving the triggering events helps guide counseling solutions.

If the divorce process is not handled well, the consequences may be serious in the long run, but they can be avoided by looking for a counselor who guides the parties to do it as easily as possible, even though it is uncomfortable.

The role of counselors should be to create a compassionate environment in which they can provide leadership through appropriate interpersonal guidance, training on healthy coping mechanisms and adequate coordination of intensive care services. All clients should appreciate that their mental health and well-being are paramount and that resources exist to promote resilience on the journey toward emotional freedom.

V

THE COUNSELING RESPONSE: CASE STUDIES

Grief

Grief[3] is an emotional and psychological experience triggered by a significant loss. It can manifest itself in different degrees and take various forms. It can make a person feel overwhelmed and exhausted, confused and dissatisfied. It also awakens deep feelings of sadness, anger, fear, disbelief, among others.

A significant loss can occur in many ways. First, the most painful case is the death of a loved one; the breakup of a romantic relationship or friendship; divorce or separation; forced dismissal from a job; serious illness or injury; natural disasters that result in the loss of material goods, such as homes, cars, commercial properties, etc., which are personal or family assets.

The truth is that, in any case, grief can challenge a person in all aspects of their life, causing feelings of anxiety, stress, and other emotional responses. The role of the grief counselor is to help people manage these feelings caused by the traumatic event while providing support throughout their grieving process.

One of the primary functions of the grief counselor is to create a safe and empathetic environment for their clients. The person going through this circumstance may need to express their emotions and receive support in a way that allows them to talk about their thoughts and feelings.

In this treatment, it is important to bear in mind that grief is a very difficult process to navigate, one that takes time and is not always linear. Let's say that, for the purposes of psychological and spiritual counseling, it is one of the most complex tasks and must be treated with great care and empathy because, in addition, everyone reacts differently to loss, and it is never clear how they will react.

---

3. The dictionary (Merrian-Webster, n.d.) defines grief as; sorrow, grief, anguish, woe, regret mean distress of mind. Sorrow implies a sense of loss or a sense of guilt and remorse. A family united in sorrow upon the patriarch's death. Grief implies poignant sorrow for an immediate cause. The inexpressible grief of the bereaved parents. Anguish suggests torturing grief or dread. The anguish felt by the parents of the kidnapped child. Woe is deep or inconsolable grief or misery. cries of woe echoed throughout the bombed city. Regret implies pain caused by deep disappointment, fruitless longing, or unavailing remorse. nagging regret for missed opportunities.

Support should not be critical, but supportive, understanding, and compassionate. If your client is initially withdrawn, insistent, or angry during sessions, be patient, do not judge, and show a willingness to resolve problems.

Furthermore, it is good to be aware of the various stages of grief. This means familiarizing yourself with shock and denial, anger, bargaining, and depression before finally reaching acceptance. These stages of grief are a theoretical model proposed by Swiss psychiatrist Elisabeth Kübler-Ross in her book On Death and Dying, published in 1969 and widely acclaimed by readers and specialists alike. This model describes the series of phases that a person experiences in response to a significant loss, such as those mentioned at the beginning of this chapter. The five stages of grief according to Kübler-Ross are directly related to death and are described as follows:

- **Denial**: At this stage, the person feels overwhelmed and has difficulty accepting the reality of the loss. They may feel as if they are in a state of shock and may deny the seriousness of the situation.

- **Anger**: At this stage, the person experiences a sense of injustice and may feel angry at the person who has died, at God, at fate, at the world, or at their situation in general.

- **Bargaining**: At this stage, the person begins to accept the reality of the loss and tries to find ways to negotiate. They may make promises to themselves or to God to try to change how they feel and improve their attitude toward the situation.

- **Depression**: At this stage, the person feels sad and depressed. They may experience feelings of loneliness, isolation, pessimism, and may cry frequently.

- **Acceptance**: At this stage, the person begins to accept the reality of the loss and find ways to move forward, understanding that death is part of life and that, like any natural process, it must be accepted without resistance or objection. Finally, in this phase, the person may experience a sense of peace and tranquility and begin to plan for the future.

It is important to note that not everyone experiences these stages of grief in the same way or in the same order, and that the grieving process is unique to each individual.

Thus, the knowledge and skills acquired through counseling programs better prepare counselors for psychotherapy treatments. As a first rule of thumb, never underestimate the adverse effects of grief on clients and their cognitive processes. They may need to restructure their current assumptions, goals, and habits that are fundamental to putting them on the path to functional adaptation.

Since grief is a unique experience, counselors should encourage their clients to get to know themselves as they embark on this journey. They should be well trained and experienced in identifying positive coping mechanisms that their clients may find helpful in healing.

It should be noted that when dealing with a particular type of grief, it is important to be informed about the values, temperament, and personal background of the clients. As an essential component, grief counselors must reinforce the sense of self-efficacy and self-esteem of those who are grieving, as well as provide them with tools to adapt to their current relationships, circumstances, and life changes dictated by the process they are going through. By offering compassionate support, evidence-based interventions, and empathy, counselors demonstrate that they can help clients navigate through these emotionally burdensome experiences and move forward.

- **Directed prayer: how to pray**

    1. Aiming for healing or restoration of emotional wounds.

    2. Based on acceptance of God's will.

    3. Asking for restoration of wounded emotions.

- **Bibliotherapy: books or scriptures**

Quotes: Psalm 23:4; John 14:1-6; Romans 14:8; 1 Thessalonians 4:13-14; Titus 3:7-8; Revelation 21:4; 1 Peter 5:7; 1 Peter 1:21; 2 Corinthians 1:3-4; Matthew 5:4; 2 Corinthians 5:6-8; 2 Thessalonians 2:16-17; Jeremiah 29:11; Psalm 147:3; 34:18.

Six-week action plan for counseling sessions.

Week	Action
1.	Explain the grieving process
2.	Study the Holy Scriptures
3.	Find information about managing anger caused by loss
4	What is depression and how can it be treated?
5.	How can you find the path to acceptance?
6.	How can you pray when grieving?

- **Modeling: biblical examples with case studies.**

King David loses his son. Review the story, analyze it, and apply it to the current situation with the client.

- **Social learning: information related to the case.**

    1. Grief cycle.

    2. Extended grief cycle.

    3. Anger management.

- **Mentors:** people to visit/accountability.
- **Support groups/church.**
- **References and resources:** psychologists, psychiatrists, community support groups, etc.

EXERCISE ON THE GRIEF CYCLE

Using the elements of the grief cycle and Kübler-Ross, explain how you would use them in different cases of loss.

- Loss of a loved one:

  _____

- Loss of a relationship:

  _____

- Loss of a son or daughter:

  _____

Suicide

Suicide is a serious mental health problem, responsible for approximately 800,000 deaths each year worldwide. Although there is significant variation in terms of age, gender, and location of those most affected by suicidal ideation, this scourge remains a major public health issue, especially among vulnerable populations.

As counselors, it is our responsibility to be equipped with the knowledge and skills necessary to identify suicide risk factors, provide appropriate interventions and support, and promote positive mental and emotional health among our clients.

One of the primary roles of a counselor, in this case and in all cases, is to develop a strong, empathetic relationship with those at risk of suicide and enable them to access appropriate care quickly and efficiently.

We must be attentive and aware of triggering factors, such as substance abuse, mental health issues like depression, anxiety, and trauma, or suicidal thoughts. People who began to feel trapped and socially isolated could trigger depression.

In this sense, counselors must emphasize and be ready to question the client's negative thoughts associated with any outcome. Through cognitive-behavioral therapy[4] and crisis intervention theories[5], counselors tend to develop communication patterns that consider paying open and nonjudgmental attention to reveal the suicidal nature of their thoughts. Second, they must be knowledgeable about suicide prevention strategies, as well as be well-versed in teaching their clients healthy and adaptive coping mechanisms when identifying the need for further attention.

Appropriate options could range from psychotherapy treatments, such as cognitive behavioral therapy, to intervention and medication from a psychiatrist. Counselors should encourage their clients to meet with therapists who take an individualized approach.

Finally, as counselors, we must identify suicidal ideation as a problem that affects not only the individual, but also their networks and the community at large.

To address this problem at a systemic level, we must partner with healthcare providers, lawyers, social workers, and other professionals involved in public health initiatives. By partnering with schools, researchers, and policymakers, prevention strategies can be offered to create safe community environments and promote mental well-being.

In conclusion, counselors are essential partners in the fight against suicide. Our roles are becoming increasingly crucial due to the rise in incidents resulting from various negative social perceptions. By remaining actively involved, attentive, and supportive of our clients, we can ensure that individuals struggling with suicidal thoughts receive

---

4. Cognitive behavioral therapy (CBT) is a therapeutic approach based on the idea that thoughts, emotions, and behaviors are interrelated and that changing one of these components can affect the others. CBT focuses on identifying the patterns of thinking and behavior that contribute to emotional problems and working to change them through the acquisition of new skills. In cognitive behavioral therapy, the therapist works with the patient to identify and challenge negative or irrational thoughts that contribute to the emotional problem. Once these thoughts are identified, the therapist helps the patient replace them with more realistic and positive thoughts. In addition, techniques are taught to modify behaviors that may be contributing to the problem, such as avoiding stressful situations or adopting unhealthy sleep patterns. CBT is used to treat a wide variety of emotional problems such as depression, anxiety, eating disorders, post-traumatic stress, and personality disorders. In addition, it has been shown to be an effective and short-term treatment compared to other therapeutic approaches.

5. Crisis intervention theories are therapeutic approaches used to help people cope with crisis situations. These theories focus on providing short-term support and guidance to help people overcome the crisis and return to normal functioning. Some crisis intervention theories include:
Roberts' crisis intervention model: focuses on assessing the crsis situation and identifying strategies to resolve the problem.
The psychological approach to crisis: focuses on understanding the psychological processes that occur during a crisis and identifying strategies to help the person overcome it.
Resilience theory: focuses on promoting the person's ability to recover from a crisis and strengthening their ability to cope with stressful situations in the future.
Positive reassessment theory: focuses on identifying positive aspects of the crisis situation and building a positive perspective to help the person overcome it.
These therapeutic approaches are commonly used to treat crisis situations, such as the loss of a loved one, domestic violence, job loss, or substance abuse.

appropriate intervention and access to the resources necessary to promote positive mental and emotional health. Additional education on suicide prevention[6], collaborative outreach, consistent assessment, and adaptation show that they are equipped to overcome this mental health giant.

- **Directed prayer: how to pray**

Three main areas of prayer.

1. Shame and guilt.

2. Forgiveness.

3. Inner healing.

- **Bibliotherapy: books or scriptures**

Quotes: Psalm 46:1; Romans 10:13; Hebrews 7:25; 1 Peter 5:7.

---

6. Suicide prevention is a complex process involving a variety of strategies, some of which include:
Promoting public awareness about suicide and associated risk factors.
Providing education about mental health and suicide prevention in schools and in the community.
Identifying and appropriately treating mental health disorders, such as depression and anxiety.
Providing adequate and timely access to mental health services and treatment for those who need it.
Developing support programs for people who have lost someone to suicide.
Encouraging open communication and social support for those at risk of suicide. Implement safety measures to limit access to means of suicide, such as restricting access to firearms or toxic substances.
Identify and support those at higher risk of suicide, such as people with a history of suicide attempts or mental health disorders.
Train health professionals and other service providers to identify and appropriately treat people at risk of suicide.

Six-week action plan for counseling sessions

Week	Action
1.	Risk factors
2.	Discuss "whether you want to commit suicide"
3.	Discuss "how to help a friend"
4.	Depression
5.	Myths about suicide
6.	How to pray?

- **Modeling**: biblical examples with case studies: Apostle Judas vs. Apostle Peter.
- **Social learning**: information related to the case study.
- **Mentors:** people to visit / accountability.
- **Support groups / church.**
- **References and resources.**

Divorce

Divorce is a complex issue that often involves significant emotional, financial, and legal challenges. Both parties lose significant emotional support, and awareness of issues such as alienation amplifies negative traits. Although divorce can offer a fresh start and provide much-needed relief from problems resulting from marital issues or dissatisfaction, it has a significant impact on mental health.

As counselors, in addition to providing support, it is necessary to understand that people going through divorce face emotional and psychological challenges, such as anxiety, depression, stress, sudden lifestyle changes, and access to support resources during such transitions.

A critical function of counseling in divorce management is to provide a supportive and empathetic environment, without judging those seeking therapy. Part of this process is recognizing the complexity of living through these challenges, avoiding oversimplifying problems, and refraining from condemning such clients. Counselors should try to understand their experiences before jumping to conclusions.

Providing encouragement and listening attentively and sensitively provides crucial guidance for identifying solutions. Professionals should minimize the labeling of those affected, which is generated by a society of which both parties are undoubtedly aware in theory, through the nonviolent communication skills dictated by relationship counseling techniques.

Second, since divorce is a unique experience that affects each person differently, counselors should use relevant and effective counseling methodologies during the therapeutic process, such as narrative and solution-focused counseling or cognitive therapy techniques.

Using counseling techniques, deeply rooted problems underlying marital conflicts can be identified. By creating open behavior, listening genuinely, and carefully reviewing the client's perceptions, alternative perspectives are revealed and the long-term risk associated with typical generalized mental health predispositions is manifested.

Finally, while guiding individuals through divorce is crucial, counselors must also provide coping strategies on how both parties can adjust to their new lives after completing the legal processes related to divorce and beyond. Ideally, they should be provided with essential healing practices, such as stress management, healthier approaches to communication, and support systems outside of the broken relationship. The counselor could align them with community programs or mental health treatments, such as inpatient and outpatient counseling for patients who are finding the transition difficult.

In summary, divorce presents many emotional and mental health challenges that require professional attention. Both parties struggle with significant issues, so understanding each other's perspective and reliving the triggering events helps guide counseling solutions. It is important to understand that, if not handled well, separation can have serious long-term consequences that can be avoided by seeking a counselor.

A compassionate environment must be created in which support is provided through appropriate interpersonal guidance, training on healthy coping mechanisms, and proper coordination of intensive medical care services. It must appreciate that a supportive environment must be created in which support is provided through appropriate interpersonal guidance, training on healthy coping mechanisms, and proper coordination of intensive care services.

Divorce and remarriage

- **Guided prayer: how to pray**

    1. Healing.

    2. Acceptance of God's will.

    3. Restoration.

- **Bibliotherapy**: books or scriptures

    1. Chapman, G. D. (2004). The Five Love Languages. Chicago, IL: Unilit Publishing.

2. Chapman, G. D. (2010). The Five Love Languages: Men's Edition. Barcelona, Spain: Editorial Unilit.

3. Dobson, J. (1983). Love Must Be Tough. Dallas, TX: Word Publishing.

4. Jakes, T. D. (2008). Before You Do Anything (1st ed.). New York, NY: Atria Books.

5. Wheat, E., & Perkins, G. O. (1980). Love life: for every married couple. Grand Rapids, MI: Zondervan Publishing House.

- Quotes: Matthew 5:31-32; 19:3-12; 1 Corinthians 7:1-40; Romans 7:2; 2 Corinthians 6:14-16.

Six-week action plan for counseling sessions

Session	Action
1.	Establishing relationships and discovering problematic emotional areas
2.	Explain the cycle of grief
3.	Self-esteem
4.	Power and control wheel
5.	What to look for in a Christian spouse
6.	How to pray?

- **Modeling:** Review biblical examples, such as Job, who suffered the loss of his family, or King David, who lost his newborn son, etc.

- **Social learning:** Information related to the case.

- **Mentors:** People to visit/accountability.

- **Support groups/church.**

- **References and resources.**

Substance abuse

This is a complex problem that has far-reaching effects on individuals, families, and communities. As counselors, it is essential that we have a deep understanding of the factors that contribute to substance abuse, the impact it has on the individual, and knowledge of the different effective treatment approaches.

The root causes of substance abuse are complex and multifaceted. Personality traits, such as impulsivity and sensation seeking, combined with genetic and environmental factors, can increase a person's risk of developing a substance use disorder. Traumatic experiences, mental health disorders, and socioeconomic factors can also play a significant role in the development of substance abuse problems.

Regardless of the underlying causes, substance abuse has serious consequences for individuals and their loved ones. Prolonged substance use can cause physical health disorders, such as liver damage and cognitive impairment. It can also lead to dysfunctional personal relationships, financial difficulties, and legal problems, such as arrest and incarceration. The negative repercussions of substance abuse extend beyond the individual and cause harm to society as a whole.

The ultimate goal of a counselor working with people struggling with substance use disorders is to help them overcome their addiction. However, there can be many challenges along the way, as they may deny they have an addiction, resist treatment, or struggle with relapse. Addressing these issues requires being equipped with a variety of therapeutic tools.

One of the most effective intervention strategies in the treatment of substance abuse is cognitive behavioral therapy (CBT), which focuses on identifying and modifying the thoughts and behaviors that contribute to substance abuse. CBT can help people identify the triggers for substance use and develop coping mechanisms to manage stress and chemical dependency. Motivational interviewing is another technique used by counselors to help individuals explore their ambivalence about change and increase their motivation to work toward sobriety.

To support long-term recovery, a holistic approach that addresses all aspects of the individual's life, including physical health, social support, and spiritual well-being, must also be incorporated. Engage with peer support groups and participate in activities that promote mental and physical well-being. In addition, family members and loved ones should be involved in the treatment process to provide a supportive and caring environment for the person in recovery.

In conclusion, substance abuse is a complex issue that requires individualized attention. Substance use disorders have significant implications for the individual, their loved ones, and society. As counselors, we must be aware of the causal factors and consequences of substance abuse. We use evidence-based interventions to provide an appropriate course of treatment for the affected individual. Understanding the complex reasons behind addiction and utilizing effective treatment options can help achieve and maintain long-term recovery.

Pornography Addiction

Pornography addiction is a growing problem that affects many in today's society. It can have negative effects on an individual's physical, emotional, and psychological well-being, as well as on their social relationships. As counselors, it is important that we understand the root causes of pornography addiction and provide effective treatment to help those affected overcome this addiction.

The factors contributing to pornography addiction are complex and often multifaceted. Some common origins include trauma, stress, anxiety, depression, and a lack of healthy emotional connection in personal relationships. In addition, those struggling with this issue have reported that social isolation and overwork are possible triggers. These causes can be exacerbated by environmental and cultural factors, such as the prevalence of explicit material and ease of access to it.

The negative repercussions of pornography addiction can vary from person to person. In some cases, it can lead to distorted perceptions of sex, which, in turn, eventually leads to poor romantic relationships. Others may experience physical effects, such as fatigue, lack of productivity, and self-loathing. One of the crucial aspects of helping those struggling with this type of addiction is awareness of the effects it can have on their journey toward healthy relationships and a fulfilling lifestyle.

Often, this disorder cannot be addressed solely through abstinence from pornography, as individuals may be using it to escape underlying psychological or emotional issues. Identifying and treating these issues is essential for long-term recovery.

Effective treatments for pornography addiction may include individual therapy with a trained counselor and joining a support group. Some approaches may benefit from creating a functional plan that involves a combination of strategies, such as establishing accountability for the addiction, improving rest and self-care practices, and ultimately reconnecting socially and emotionally with people more deeply.

Counselors can use a number of evidence-based therapeutic techniques to help people overcome pornography addiction. Again, cognitive behavioral therapy (CBT) is one such approach that can help them recognize and change the thought patterns that contribute to the situation. During sessions, they are asked to identify their thought patterns, engage in self-reflection on how these thoughts and behaviors contribute to impulsive decisions, and proceed to modify them, guided by a series of methods that may be appropriate. Mindfulness exercises and meditation may also be used to help them focus their mental energy on the present and engage in healthy coping mechanisms.

Another important aspect of treating pornography addiction is fostering resilience and social interaction. Reinforcing a sense of community and positive reinforcement could play an essential role in creating conditions for broad behavioral and lifestyle change. Participation in social activities that are positive in nature can result in a valuable support system.

In summary, pornography addiction is a complex phenomenon that requires specialized counseling and therapy to address. Understanding the factors that can lead to addiction, recognizing the negative consequences, and finding the most appropriate treatment are key to helping those affected achieve a fulfilling life. The use of useful and effective evidence-based strategies can be successful in encouraging healthier behaviors, promoting emotional well-being, and caution with regard to attraction to such materials. As counselors, it is our obligation to stay informed about best practices and work to help people struggling with pornography addiction achieve long-term success.

EXERCISE ON THE TWELVE STEPS OF ADDICTION

How would you apply them to a group counseling plan?

- Substance addiction:

_____

- Pornography addiction:

_____

It is necessary to confess, acknowledge, and be willing.

- We admitted that we were powerless over addiction, that our lives had become unmanageable.

- We came to believe that a power greater than ourselves could restore us to sanity.

- We decided to turn our will and our lives over to the care of God as we understood Him.

- Without fear, we made a searching and fearless moral inventory of ourselves.

- We admitted to God, to ourselves, and to another human being the exact nature of our faults.

- We were entirely ready to have God remove all these character defects from us.

- We humbly asked Him to remove our shortcomings.

- We made a list of all persons we had harmed and became willing to make amends to them all.

- We made direct amends to as many as we could, except when doing so would harm them or others.

- We continued to take personal inventory and when we were wrong, we admitted it immediately.

- Through prayer and meditation, we seek to improve our conscious contact with God, as we understand Him, asking only that He let us know His will for us and give us the strength to carry it out.

- Having gained spiritual awakening as a result of these steps, we try to carry this message to other alcoholics and practice these principles in all our affairs.

Abortion

Abortion remains one of the most divisive and controversial issues around the world. Opinions on this topic are often determined by philosophical, religious, social, and moral beliefs. As counselors, it is important that we provide emotional support, unbiased information, and guidance to individuals facing the difficult decision of terminating their pregnancy.

One of the first things women considering abortion should do is seek counseling and medical information. This should include discussions about the physical, psychological, and emotional aspects of terminating a pregnancy. Prior consultation on the subject can help them understand the procedure, potential risks, and side effects, and prepare them for the experience.

Counselors play an important role in preparing those who plan to have an abortion. This may involve helping them process each and every emotion associated with their decision. An abortion can be a traumatic experience for some, so it is important for clients to understand that there is no guarantee of how they will feel after having an abortion.

The counseling process can help women identify, acknowledge, and overcome any feelings of guilt, shame, or loss they may experience after the procedure. Counselors should also suggest that they work with healthcare professionals specializing in gynecology to better understand the procedure that will be used and to learn about possible complications.

It is important for counselors to remain neutral, without jargon or judgment, and to provide the necessary information about the procedure. They should take into account that this may include possible complications, recovery periods, and other aspects that may not be highlighted elsewhere. Pre-procedure counseling can help clients make the best decision for themselves.

Counselors should also provide individuals with information about alternatives for unplanned pregnancies. Some individuals may not be fully aware of options, such as adoption, which can provide a safe and loving home for an unborn child. Counselors should remain neutral in this regard and provide credible information to enable them to make an informed decision about which path to take.

In conclusion, pre-abortion counseling plays a fundamental role in providing support and guidance to women who are planning to undergo an abortion. The goal should be to provide an enriching experience that helps them understand and make informed decisions. Professionals must remain impartial in their methods and provide verified information about the risks and benefits of abortion. Ultimately, any decision related to abortion must depend entirely and solely on the individual. The role of the counselor is to provide advice that allows them to make the best and most informed choice based on their individual circumstances.

- **Guided prayer: how to pray**

Three main areas of prayer.

1. Shame and guilt.

2. Forgiveness.

3. Inner healing.

- **Bibliotherapy:** books or scriptures

Book to recommend before an abortion is performed:

1. Sandvig, Karen J. (1988). You're what? Help and hope for pregnant teens. Ventura, CA: Regal.

Recommended book after an abortion has been performed:

2. Nykiel, Connie (2001). No one told me I could cry. Lewiston, NY: Life Cycle Books.

Bible verses to work on before the abortion:

Jeremiah 1:5; Zephaniah 3:17; Psalm 139:13-16.

Bible verses to work on after the abortion:

Psalm 132:1; Mark 4:12; Lamentations 3:22-24.

Six-week action plan for counseling sessions

Before abortion	After abortion
1. Alternatives to abortion	1. Grief cycle, session I
2. Medical procedures	2. Grief cycle, session II
3. Psychological effects	3. Managing emotions
4. Communication	4. Future plans and goals
5. Sex education	5. Where to get help
6. How to pray	6. How to pray

- **Modeling:** biblical examples.
- **Social learning:** information related to the case.
- **Mentors:** people to visit/accountability.
- **Support groups/church.**
- **References and resources.**

Violence against women

Violence against women is a serious problem that affects many nations around the world. It has multiple layers and complex dimensions: cultural, social, psychological, economic, and political. As counselors, we play an important role in recognizing this situation and helping to address it, especially by identifying those who suffer from it and offering them appropriate treatment with absolute empathy.

Awareness and sensitivity to domestic violence must be our first line of action. This is essential, given the tendency of victims of violence to remain silent and mask or trivialize the abuse they endure. A counselor must understand that the external representation of abuse is only a small part of the aggression that is demonstrated. The effect of violence on women is much deeper and manifests itself in lifelong psychological struggles that cause fear, anxiety, and abandonment issues. Therefore, counselors strive to stay up to date on best practices for recognizing signs of violence against women, sensitizing victims, and holding perpetrators accountable.

We can help women realize that experiencing violence is never acceptable or inevitable. Encouraging open conversations about abuse, highlighting personal boundaries, safety preparedness, and empowering women has proven useful in promoting awareness, defending those affected, and starting the conversation in societies about respect for women.

Counselors must be well trained so as not to downplay the situation or even suggest that it is somehow the woman's fault. Such behavior only risks exacerbating the ambivalent feelings of shame and guilt that the victim already experiences.

We must be aware of the power and control dynamics at play in cases of domestic violence. Victims of abuse often feel trapped and frightened in a dynamic in which their power has been taken away by force and replaced by the abuser's total control. It is common for the abuser to isolate, intimidate, and manipulate their victim to get what they want. As professionals, we need to recognize this power dynamic and work to empower clients who may feel powerless, distressed, and under the total control of the other person.

Finally, it is essential that we take an active approach when we discover that someone we are working with may be at risk of violence. Counselors must establish safe connections with these women and assess the situation while working with them on violence prevention.

When a woman is found to be at risk, strategies should be introduced to promote her empowerment and reduce the danger. These may include developing safety plans and identifying safe places in case of an emergency. Interagency collaboration, developing support networks, reporting to local authorities, and arranging alternative accommodation, among other initiatives, could be used to ensure that support is available.

In summary, violence against women is a scourge that must be addressed. Counselors have an important role to play in recognizing and addressing this problem by staying informed about best practices for raising awareness, monitoring, and ensuring accountability.

It is also essential to raise awareness about boundaries, encourage conversations about abuse, and consider the power dynamics in abusive relationships. Counselors should not shy away from taking the necessary steps to protect women at risk of violence.

Psychological or sexual abuse/rape against women

- Targeted prayer: how to pray

    1. Healing.

    2. Forgiveness.

    3. Restoration.

    4. Guilt/shame.

    5. Fear.

- Bibliotherapy: books or scriptures

Quotes: Luke 6:36-37; 17:3; Mark 11:25; Matthew 6:14-15; Colossians 3:13; 2 Corinthians 2:10; Joel 2:26-27; Isaiah 50:6-9; Jude 1:24; Jeremiah 30:17; Psalms 23:3; 147:20; Zechariah 9:12; Isaiah 53:5; 2 Corinthians 5:17; John 16:33; Isaiah 35:4; Philippians 4:6-7; Colossians 3:15; Matthew 18:1-14.

Six-week action plan for counseling sessions

Weeks	Actions
1.	Self-forgiveness
2.	Depression
3.	Suicide
4.	Identity
5.	Confrontation skills
6.	Relationship building

- **Modeling**: **Biblical examples with case studies.**

    The case of Tamar, which appears in 2 Samuel 13:2.

- **Social learning.**

    1. Coping skills.

    2. Building a relationship.

    3. Power and control wheel.

- **Mentors:** Be accountable to someone.
- **Support groups/church.**
- **References and resources.**

EXERCISE ON THE CIRCLE OF POWER AND CONTROL AS BIBLIOTHERAPY

Define the elements of the circle of power and control and develop a six-week program using the elements.

- Male privilege:

- Threats:

- Intimidation:

- Emotional abuse:

- Isolation:

- Devaluing, denying, and blaming:

- Manipulation of sons and daughters:

- Economic abuse:

Sexual identity and gender

Sexual identity is an important aspect of a person's wholeness. It refers to one's sense of self as an individual and how they identify with regard to their sexual orientation and gender. As counselors, we play a critical role in supporting clients on their sexual identity journey.

One of the most important things professionals can do is work to create a safe, nonjudgmental space for clients to explore their sexual identity. This type of open environment can build trust between the counselor and the client and create a compelling relationship that can lead to significant progress in self-discovery.

In this sense, dialogue and education are key components of this type of work, providing clients with a space to fully express themselves and allowing counselors to help them better understand what they are going through.

Many people seek counseling while grappling with their sexual identity. To do this, counselors need to be knowledgeable about different sexual orientations and their impact on the psyche of those who identify with them. This may involve asking open-ended questions that allow them to describe their experiences rather than offering help in categorizing them.

Within coping strategies, counselors can also work to change ideologies through the use of exposure therapy and encourage men or women who expect conformity and gender rigidity to foster a greater "understanding that there is no one-size-fits-all format for human life."

Counselors can also help clients anticipate potential challenges and the impact their decisions could have on their self-esteem throughout their lives.

It is expected that some family members, colleagues, and friends will not understand an individual's preferences, causing them to feel isolated and alone. Counselors can play a very important role in helping to develop coping strategies to mitigate these feelings.

An excellent tool known as affirmative counseling can be used, as it does not rigidly adhere to a particular counseling method and satisfactorily accommodates clients exclusively in what is requested.

Affirmative counseling chooses therapy that instills a spiritual, practical, psychological, or behavioral roadmap that meets clients where they feel they embody their journey to any point. With their agreement, therapists could educate them about specialized care, alternative means of support, or community resources, and monitor depression, anxiety, substance abuse, or self-harm tendencies in coping mechanisms that arise from gender identification pathology.

In conclusion, sexual identity is a critical aspect of a person's life that can greatly influence their mental and emotional well-being. As counselors, we have a responsibility to ensure that all clients of different sexual preferences, orientations, identities, and lifestyles have access to safe and supportive resources to better understand what they are experiencing.

Sexual identity or gender

- **Guided prayer:** how to pray

    1. Rejection.

    2. Forgiveness/restoration.

    3. Rebellion.

    4. Loneliness.

    5. Salvation.

- **Bibliotherapy: books or scriptures**

Exodus Project.

References: 1 John 1:9; Leviticus 20:13; 1 Corinthians 6:9-11; Genesis 1:28; 2:24; 1 Timothy 1:8-10; Romans 1:26-27; Galatians 5:16; Mark 11:25; Luke 17:3-4; Colossians 3:13; 2 Corinthians 7:9-10; Jude 1:7; Psalm 34:18.

Six-week action plan for counseling sessions

Weeks	Action
1.	Repentance
2.	Self-forgiveness
3.	Depression
4.	Suicide
5.	Issues of identity and biblical roles
6	Christian life

- **Modeling:** Biblical examples with case studies.
  Sodom and Gomorrah
- **Social learning.**
- **Mentors:** Be accountable to someone.
- **Support groups/church.**
- **References and resources.**

VI

REAL-LIFE CASES OF APLIED COUNSELING

We have reached the end, and I want to confess to you, dear reader, that writing this book has been a wonderful experience. Looking back on the things I have learned throughout my life and the interactions that have shaped me, I now know that they continue to be cathartic and quite satisfying for me.

Counseling has been a powerful tool that has changed the lives of many and, in this case, my own. Throughout my personal journey, I have made significant adjustments to my practice that, in my opinion, have made me a better human being and a more effective counselor.

Well, I want to share three of these experiences in this last chapter. At the end of each story, I include an exercise to help with the application of what has been learned.

The first is based on a six-week counseling program I conducted at the University of Texas Counseling Center. A middle-aged woman came to the center for grief counseling, and the sessions impacted my life regarding the critical importance of ethics in counseling. The second is based on post-abortion counseling sessions I had with a young woman in her thirties. I was already a pastor and presented myself to her as a pastoral counselor. The experience affirmed my belief that in some critical cases, a religious solution is needed for people's spiritual needs.

The third case involved counseling I did with a young man in his thirties who was trying with all his might to overcome his drug addiction. The interesting thing about that experience is that it helped me develop the need for a comprehensive approach to counseling.

Without further ado, here is a more detailed description of each of these experiences. I hope you find it useful in your journey as a counselor.

First experience: Grief and ethics

The university counseling center had scheduled me to help a middle-aged woman who had recently lost her elderly mother. Her life was typical of a Hispanic woman in South Texas. She was happily married and had three adult children. I assumed it would be relatively easy to help her cope with her grief. I thought she had dealt with the initial shock of her mother's death and would now participate in a prescribed six-week counseling program typical of the Kübler-Ross grief cycle. But I was wrong.

My first mistake was making assumptions about her condition and feelings. I remembered my university professors who often taught me to avoid making any assumptions until treatment had begun. The thing is, assumptions can lead us in the wrong direction. I was also overconfident in my abilities and believed that my training was sufficient to help this client with her needs.

I soon discovered that the woman was still quite distressed over her mother's death. Her feelings were still very raw, and it seemed to me that she was not processing the event in a healthy way. The typical grief cycle had to wait while I tried to understand where her pain was coming from.

From our initial conversations, I concluded that there were obviously some serious unresolved issues between this daughter and her mother. Although her death was due to a long-term illness, underlying family issues that went back to her childhood had not been addressed.

What made counseling more complex was the fact that she needed forgiveness. She needed to forgive herself for things that were beyond her control and forgive her mother for her voluntary and perhaps involuntary or inadvertent participation.

Psychology perceives forgiveness as the voluntary release of feelings or resentment toward a person or persons who have hurt us. While I find the exercise good and useful, I find it very difficult without the spiritual component. Since I was in a secular (non-Christian) environment, I did not have the freedom to inject or use any kind of spiritual or Christian element in the counseling sessions. I completely respect this ethic, even though I was trying to help this woman without the benefit of a spiritual basis for forgiveness.

Now, even though I was not allowed to bring my spiritual or Christian perspective into the counseling session, I had been taught, appropriately, that if a client voluntarily mentioned their beliefs in the session or expressed them, then I could use that context to help them deal with their problems from a place of faith. When I began to talk to her about forgiveness, she immediately understood the concept from her Christian perspective. In her case, the power of forgiveness became more powerful than the cycle of grief.

It was essential that I do not bring my Christian beliefs into the counseling sessions, because I could offend theirs. Likewise, my belief system could compromise their perception of my ability to help. It is essential that a counselor keep their beliefs to themselves until they understand their client's persuasion.

Now, if you are a Christian counselor in a Christian counseling setting, you would be understood and even expected to do so. However, it is helpful to allow your client to guide you toward the best course of action for them.

Exercise

Define the following ethical terms and apply them to grief.

- Ethics:

- Familiarity with the law:

- Client contact:

- Dual relationships:

- Confidentiality: Referrals:

- Record keeping:

- Competence and referral:

Source: Sharf, R. S. (2000). Theories of psychotherapy and counseling: Concepts and cases. Brooks/Cole-Thomson Learning.

Second experience:
Abortion and a Christian perspective

I know that abortion is a very divisive issue in our time, but a counselor cannot afford to choose easy cases.

A young woman in her twenties made an appointment for counseling at my church office. She had been experiencing severe depression and a great deal of anxiety. She seemed quite distressed.

With the help of her boyfriend, about ten years earlier, she had had an abortion. Many nights she cried herself to sleep, feeling painful guilt—in her words—for taking her baby's life.

She often heard a baby crying. On the anniversary of her abortion, she would look for children who were the same age as her unborn son and say to herself, "This is how old my baby boy would be." To make matters worse, her despair increased because she had just discovered she had breast cancer.

Post-abortion counseling is one of the most difficult types of counseling a counselor will ever face. When the time comes, you will be ready with counseling plans and strategies to help ease the pain and allow the person to move forward, but you never know what might happen.

Although I was trained to separate myself from the pain or emotions of any counseling situation, I found these cases very challenging. This one, in particular, completely changed my counseling perspectives and practices. The experience strongly affirmed my belief that in some critical cases, a religious solution is needed for people's spiritual needs. Since then, I have been convinced that psychology helps us define our problems, but the Bible gives us the solutions to those problems.

Forgiveness was my primary concern. However, this client could not forgive herself due to the mental health aspects of her condition. Whether due to a religious background or a natural reaction, she was condemning herself for her actions and feared for her life because she expressed suicidal thoughts.

So, I was compelled to recommend professional psychiatric help to alleviate her depression and anxiety from a medical standpoint. Once she stabilized, I was able to begin hel- ping her with the spiritual aspect of her guilt.

It is important to seek medical or psychiatric help when warranted. Remember, counseling is for healthy people who are trying to cope with normal life events.

If someone has a chemical imbalance or psychiatric problems, counseling could do more harm than good. Be careful to refer people you believe need medical or psychiatric help as soon as possible.

Once I was satisfied that she had normalized, I asked her to return and began to help her deal with her guilt. As she was a practicing Christian, I helped her focus on Jesus' sacrifice and how the Master could forgive her so she could begin a process of forgiving herself.

After several counseling sessions, I encouraged her to join a support group with people who, like her, needed help and ongoing supervision. Today, I am happy to say that she is doing well! She survived cancer, remarried, and started a new family. She lives with the expectation that she will see her baby once she gets to heaven.

EXERCISE: REFLECT ON THE DIFFERENCES WITH THE ANDERSON MODEL

Secular versus Christian counseling

Biblical	Secular
Church member	Client in conflict
Church	Therapist
Problem Identification	Problem assessment
Initial ministry	Initial Intervention
Providing church support	Referral to further care
Church	Therapist
Sanctification	Ongoing treatment
Discipleship	Psychotherapy
Bible Study	Spiritual intervention
Support groups	Medical care
Resolution and service	

Source: Anderson, N. T. D.Min., Zuehlke, T. E., Ph.D., & Zuehlke, J. S. (2000). Christ-centered therapy. Grand Rapids, MI: Zondervan Publishing House – Harper Collins Publishers.

Third experience: From drug addict to pastor

The third case was a tumultuous counseling season with a young Christian man in his thirties who was trying with all his might to kick his drug addiction. His story compelled me to develop the need for a comprehensive approach to counseling. The final journey to recovery required individual, family, and divine interventions.

Alcohol was the gateway drug that led this young man to the brink of despair. He suggested that he would never have touched cocaine if he hadn't been drunk. Later, he became a functional drug user. Because he was alternating between work and school, he initially thought he could control his impulses and enjoy drugs recreationally.

Eventually, as expected, the drugs became impossible to control. In the worst cases, he began to go on three-day binges that sent his personal and family life into a spiral of despair. Family, friends, and church became irrelevant as drugs took control. After several years of abuse, several changes of location, and after being on the verge of losing his family, he was open and ready to receive help.

The initial concern is the need for personal growth and the development of the young person's identity with himself and with God. Young people make significant mistakes in their lives because they are searching for identity, self-esteem, and purpose. Through a series of interventions, this client was able to make the heartbreaking decision to get help. Only when a person is clear about who he is and where he wants to go is he able to go through the pain of sobriety.

Counseling and self-discovery allowed forgiveness and love to nourish his spirit and give him the power to overcome. The Holy Spirit became his source of power, the power that freed him and sustained him even in his darkest days, and that would become the supernatural motivation that would guide him toward self-control and, ultimately, victory.

After his long journey and years of sobriety, the young man finished his studies, became a pastor of a Christian church, and a university professor of history. Today, he is a traveling lecturer and head of the History Department at the college where he teaches. This case confirmed my theoretical tendencies in social psychology as described by Dr. Alfred Adler. It truly takes the support of an extended family and a church community for someone to regain their health and social functioning.

In conclusion, I want to introduce you to my personal counseling model. I pray it is helpful in your service to your community.

Introduction to the Counseling Model
Integral Biblical Development (IBD) by Dr. Steven Benavides

"EVERY ACT OF FAITH REQUIRES DISCIPLINE."

The IBD model assumes that human beings are tripartite. Specifically, we are an entity composed of: (1) a spirit, which comes from God; (2) a soul, which is composed of emotions, conscience, and will; and finally, (3) a physical body. A counseling model can improve any part or area of the human being and utilize the healing properties intrinsic to the image of God in every part of our spiritual and physical essence.

Counseling lives in the areas of the soul that affect emotions and, in its ability, to shape consciousness and move or enable the human will to change. The spirit of the human being is primarily affected by the affective and cognitive relationship of a religious experience or encounter.

The ecclesial context is the area where God gives himself the right to live actively in human beings. If a man or woman chooses not to have a religious-spiritual life, they lose the ability to be empowered by the Holy Spirit and by the power of the Bible as a compass for conscience and morality. Finally, the body, with its healing powers, must be part of therapies that focus not only on the soul, but also on the physical body's ability to promote health and well-being.

The IBD model is based on Dr. Jay Adams' Nouthetic counseling. This type of reality therapy requires an active role for the counselor, who must also use physical therapies to stimulate the healing capacities of the human body.

This holistic approach is not only spirit-soul-body but also requires an element of discipline. The discipline of prayer and meditation is the complement that empowers human beings to achieve victory in their therapies. It is not enough to bring about change, but also to empower for change. The combination of Adler, Adams, and a discipline of prayer or ecclesial meditation form a comprehensive counseling approach that helps in all aspects of a good counseling plan. Without further ado, the structure of the IBD model is presented below:

Counseling Model
Integral Biblical Development by Dr. Steven Benavides

Spirit, Soul, and Body Counseling

- 1 Thessalonians 5:23; Hebrews 4:12.

Soul Counseling

- 2 Timothy 3:16-17: confront with love.
- 1 Corinthians 4:14: interest in the person.
- Acts 20:31: require change.
- Supervised prayer and meditation program.

Personal prayer and fasting program

Exercise and diet program for the body

- Reduces stress.
- Helps treat anxiety.
- Strengthens the senses to avoid depression.
- Helps develop self-esteem.
- Helps with sleep.

Right relationship with God and the Church for the spirit

- Prayer, fasting, and intimacy.
- Forgiveness and freedom.
- Relational healing.
- Under pastoral supervision.

References

Adams, J. E. (1989). *Matrimonio, divorcio y nuevo matrimonio*. Clie.

Adams, J. E. (1992). *The christian counselor's manual: The practice of nouthetic counseling*. Bethany Book House.

Adams, J. E. (2002). *Competent to counsel: Introduction to nouthetic counseling*. Zondervan Publ. House.

Anderson, N. T. (2009). *Christ-centered therapy: The practical integration of theology and psychology*. Zondervan Academic.

Aranza, J. & Lamson, T. (1984). *A reasonable reason to wait: A practical guide for those who have not been sexually involved and healing for those who have*. Huntington House.

Arterburn, S. Stoeker, F., & Yorkey, M. (2010). *Every man's marriage: An every man's guide to winning the heart of a woman*. WaterVrook Press.

Arterburn, S., Stoeker, F., & Yorkey, M. (2020). *Every man's battle: Winning the war on sexual temptation one victory at a time*. WaterBrook.

Baruth, L. G., & Manning, M. L. (2012). *Multicultural counseling and psychotherapy a lifespan perspective*. Pearson/Merrill Prentice Hall.

Beer, J., Packard, C. & Stief, E. (2012b). *The mediator's handbook*. New Society.

Berg, R. C., Landreth, G. L., & Fall, K. A. (2018). *Group counseling: Concepts and procedures*. Routledge, Taylor & Francis Group.

Beyer, B. M., & Johnson, E. S. (2014). *Special programs & services in schools: Creating options, meeting needs*. Proactive Publications.

Brock, G. W., & Barnard, C. P. (2009). *Procedures in marriage and family therapy*. Pearson A and B.

Burns, D. D. (1999). *Ten days to self-esteem*. Harper.

Chapman, G. D. (2010). *The five love languages: How to express heartfelt commitment to your mate.* Manjul Pub.

[VNV], C. P. J., & [VNV], A. K. M. (2020). *Clinical management of sex addiction.* Routledge.

Clinton, T. E., & Laaser, M. R. (2010). T*he quick-reference guide to sexuality & relationship counseling.* Baker Books.

Cole, E. L. (2001). *Maximized manhood.* Whitaker House.

Comiskey, A. (1988). *Pursuing sexual wholeness.* Desert Stream Ministries.

Crabb, L. J. (1995). *The marriage builder.* Alpha.

Craig Grace, J. (n.d.). *Human development.* Prentice hall.

Dobson, J. C., & Dobson, J. C. (2001). *Complete marriage and family home reference guide.* OMF Literature.

Dobson, J. C. (2007). *Life on the edge: The next generation's guide to a meaningful future.* Tyndale House Publishers.

Dobson, J. C. (2007b). *Love must be tough.* Tynedale House.

Dobson, J. C. (1995). *Straight talk: What men need to know, what women should understand.* Word.

Drummond, R. J. (2004). *Appraisal procedures for counselors and helping professionals.* Pearson/Merrill/Prentice Hall.

Duty, G. (2002). *Divorcio y nuevo matrimonio.* Bethany House Publishers. Eisenman, R. (2020). Creativity mental illness and crime. Kendall hunt.

Gladding, S. T. (2018). *Counseling: A comprehensive profession.* Pearson Education.

Gross, C., & Harper, J. (2010). *Eyes of integrity: The porn pandemic and how it affects you.* Baker Books.

Gross, C., & Luff, S. (2010). Pure eyes: *A man's guide to sexual integrity.* Baker Books.

Gross, C., & Krummrich, C. (2006). *The dirty little secret uncovering the truth behind porn.* Zondervan.

Habermas, R. T. (2001). T*eaching for reconciliation: Foundations and practice of christian educational ministry.* Wipf and Stock.

Hawkins, R., & Clinton, T. (2009). *The quick-reference guide to biblical counseling, biblical counseling: Personal and emotional issues.* Baker Books.

Hinterkopf, E. (2015). *Integrating spirituality in counseling: A manual for using the experiential focusing method.* Jessica Kingsley Publishers.

House, A. E. (2002). *DSM-IV diagnosis in the schools.* Guilford.

James, R. K., & Gilliland, B. E. (2003). *Theories and strategies in counseling and psychotherapy.* Allyn and Bacon.

Kirk, J. R. (1985). *The mind polluters.* T. Nelson.

LaHaye, T. (2001). *How to win over depression.* Walker & Co.

LaHaye, T. (1993). *Transformed temperaments.* Living Books, Tyndale House Publishers.

McMillan, D. W. (1997). *The art of lasting relationships.* MJF.

McRoberts, D. (1976). *The hurt and healing of divorce.* D.C. Cook Pub. Co.

Schmidt, J. J. (2003). *Counseling in schools: Essential services and comprehensive programs.* Allyn and Bacon.

Schwartz, P. (1994). *Peer marriage: How love between equals really works.* Free Press.

Sharf, R. S. (2019). *Theories of psychotherapy and counseling: Concepts and cases.* Langara College.

Silverman, M., & Lustig, D. A. (2003). *Parent survival training: A complete guide to modern parenting.* MJF Books.

Smalley, G. (1996). T*he keys to growing in Love: The language of love; Love is a decision; the two sides of love.* Inspirational Press.

Somoza, D. (1992). *Fichero práctico de consejería pastoral.* Clie.

Wholey, D. (1990). *Becoming your own parent: The solution for adult children of alco- holic and other dysfunctional families.* Doubleday.

Wright, H. N. (1994). *The other woman in your marriage: Understanding a mother's impact on her son & how it affects his marriage.* Regal Books.

Made in the USA
Coppell, TX
25 February 2026